THE BATTLE OF GLENDALE

THE BATTLE OF GLENDALE

Robert E. Lee's Lost Opportunity

DOUGLAS CRENSHAW

THE History PRESS

Published by The History Press
Charleston, SC
www.historypress.net

Cover: "The Battle of Glendale" (detail), Henry Clow, County of Henrico, Virginia, Historic Preservation and Museum Services.

First published 2017

Manufactured in the United States

ISBN 978.1.62619.892.0

Library of Congress Control Number: 2016943514

Contents

Maps

Acknowledgements

I would like to thank Randy Cleaver of the Richmond National Battlefield Park (RNBP) for taking me out to the Frayser's Farm battlefield on a cold winter day when this project was just beginning. Randy was a great source of information and was very generous with his time. Bert Dunkerly also walked the battlefield with me. Mike Gorman of RNBP shared maps that he and Bob Krick created, and I found these to be the most useful of all the maps I referenced. Mike and Bert are always very supportive.

Bob Krick gave me a tremendous amount of assistance. We walked the ground together during the later stages of the project, and this provided greater clarity and insight. As the battlefield is in a completely raw state at the time of writing, it was incredibly helpful to have his assistance. Bob also opened the amazing library at RNBP to me. Anyone contemplating writing about action in the Richmond, Virginia area should absolutely make use of this resource; it contains a wealth of firsthand and secondhand sources. He also offered many suggestions to improve the book. Any errors contained within are mine alone. Bob is an extremely knowledgeable and generous person, and his assistance is greatly appreciated.

Once again, Henrico County has been very helpful and gracious in allowing me to use the paintings of Henry Clow. I would be remiss not to mention Hal Jespersen. No matter how busy Hal is, he always finds time to assist and provide his stunning maps. Thanks also to Ellen Gaglio, who has been very supportive. Thanks also to Banks Smither and Ryan Finn, my editors at The History Press. They have gone out of their way to assist me in every way possible. Finally, and most importantly, I have to thank my very patient wife, Judy. She allowed me the time to work on this project and endured many, many conversations about it.

This book is dedicated to the entire staff of the Richmond National Battlefield Park. They do important work, and they do it very well.

Prologue

Glendale. Today, it's a quiet, out-of-the-way intersection. Heavy growths of trees are on one corner, and the foundation of an old abandoned farmhouse is near the other. Across the main road, there are some woods and, a little bit in the distance, the edge of a housing development. Down one road is a pleasant country church. There is no indication that this place is different from any other country crossroad except for a few old signs. But if you drive toward the church, you will notice a small national cemetery. It seems out of place; why is it there? Something momentous happened in this lonely, peaceful spot. On the last day of June 1862, the fate of a massive Union army hung in the balance and, with it, perhaps the destiny of the Union itself. Men were slaughtered here, killed and maimed by the thousands. It was a scene of incredible terror and desperation. Time has given it a peaceful covering, but the story is powerful and right under the surface, if you merely stop and take a good look.

Chapter 1

Prelude

By the spring of 1862, things were not looking good for the Confederacy. In the west, Forts Henry, Donelson and Island No. 10 had fallen. Corinth and Memphis were lost, and the South's largest city, New Orleans, had been captured. The western army had been defeated at Shiloh, and one of the South's most promising generals, Albert Sidney Johnston, had been killed. Along the eastern coast, Jacksonville had fallen. Union troops had landed on the coast of North Carolina and captured Fort Macon. In Virginia, a massive army commanded by George B. McClellan was slowly making its way up the peninsula between the James and York Rivers. The naval yard at Norfolk had fallen, and the ironclad *Virginia* had been scuttled to prevent its capture by the Union forces. The Confederate army under Joseph E. Johnston had retreated to the outskirts of Richmond. Things appeared very dark indeed.

As McClellan's army moved ponderously toward the Confederate capital, events were occurring that would soon affect the outcome of his campaign. In the Shenandoah Valley, Thomas J. "Stonewall" Jackson led his army to a string of victories over the Union forces, causing President Lincoln to withhold a large number of troops (including part of the corps under Irvin McDowell) from McClellan. These would be stationed so that they could protect Washington against the threat posed by Jackson.

In front of Richmond, General Joseph Johnston's men prepared for the Union onslaught. A meandering swamp called the Chickahominy River posed a challenge to McClellan. Under normal conditions, it was nearly impossible

George B. McClellan. *Courtesy of the Library of Congress.*

to get infantry, artillery and wagons across it without adequate bridges. When heavy rains came, it turned into a true river. The Chickahominy lay astride McClellan's path, and he divided his army, with portions on either side. The northernmost corps under Fitz John Porter was awaiting the expected arrival of McDowell's command from the north, which, owing to Jackson, would never occur. The bulk of McClellan's army, south of the river, would be directly in front of Richmond. Confederate commander Johnston decided to take advantage of the split Union forces, and on May 31, he launched an attack against the southern portion of McClellan's army at Seen Pines (Fair Oaks). Unfortunately for the Confederacy, the attack was poorly coordinated and executed. It continued the next day with no appreciable gain but with great loss; the most important casualty was Johnston himself, who was wounded and taken from the field. President Jefferson Davis placed Robert E. Lee in command of the army at this most desperate hour.

Lee went to work immediately. He enhanced the army's supply situation, improved discipline and began reorganizing the artillery. The army's guns had been dispersed among the various divisions and brigades, diminishing the potential effectiveness of massed firepower. Lee also had extensive entrenchments built. These fortifications would not only help to protect the defenders against McClellan's infantry and artillery, but they would also allow Lee to use fewer troops to hold a position. While many derided him for this, some even referring to him as the "King of Spades" and "Granny Lee," it would prove to be a very wise decision. Because fewer troops were

Robert E. Lee. *Courtesy of the Library of Congress.*

needed to man them, the earthworks freed other troops to attack elsewhere. The Confederate commander would soon make good use of them.[1]

Lee faced other challenges besides McClellan's force—his own army was new to him. He was generally unfamiliar with the men who led his divisions and brigades and was unsure of their capabilities. It is true that he had a positive experience in planning the Valley Campaign with Jackson, with the result being a spectacular operation, but Lee's other commanders were not well known by him. How would they respond under pressure? Would they show initiative? Could they effectively organize and lead their men? Time would demonstrate that Lee had a tendency to issue orders that could be somewhat vague, leaving his subordinates room for discretion. How would his commanders respond to these? Additionally, he had a small headquarters staff. While this might seem more efficient, it would not really turn out to be so. It would become difficult for Lee to keep in touch with his sometimes widespread commanders. Lee also did not use his staff to supervise and ensure that his orders were carried out as intended. In time, of course, Lee would understand the men who served directly under him, but that was not the case in June 1862.[2]

In late June, because McDowell's corps would not be sent to join him, McClellan had only Porter's Fifth Corps stationed north of the Chickahominy protecting his supply base at White House Landing. Lee saw an opportunity. Confederate cavalry chief J.E.B. Stuart and his horsemen rode entirely around the Federal army and reported that the right wing of the enemy was "in the air," or unsupported. If Lee could strike the Union right with enough force, he could roll up McClellan's flank and drive him from his supply base. It was an audacious plan. Lee accepted the great, calculated risk and moved most of his army north of the Chickahominy, leaving his forces south of the river greatly outnumbered. If McClellan seized the opportunity there, he could crush the Confederate defenses south of the river and drive to Richmond. Were that to happen, Lee would have a difficult time getting his troops back across the river to meet the threat. He gambled correctly that McClellan would be slow to react. Lee moved the divisions of A.P. Hill, James Longstreet and D.H. Hill across the river, where they would strike McClellan at Mechanicsville. Jackson's army would come down from the Valley and move behind Porter, turning his flank. It seemed like a great, if ambitious, plan. The army was new, the commanders had not worked together for long and communications were poor. Despite these challenges, the date of the attack was set for June 26.[3]

While most of the Confederate forces were in place on time, Jackson's men were running late. It took longer than anticipated to move his army from the Shenandoah Valley to the outskirts of Richmond. The Confederates did not wait for Jackson, but instead, A.P. Hill began the assault. When Jackson did arrive in the vicinity, he was several miles away and set up camp, not taking part in the attack on the twenty-sixth. Instead of flanking the Federals and

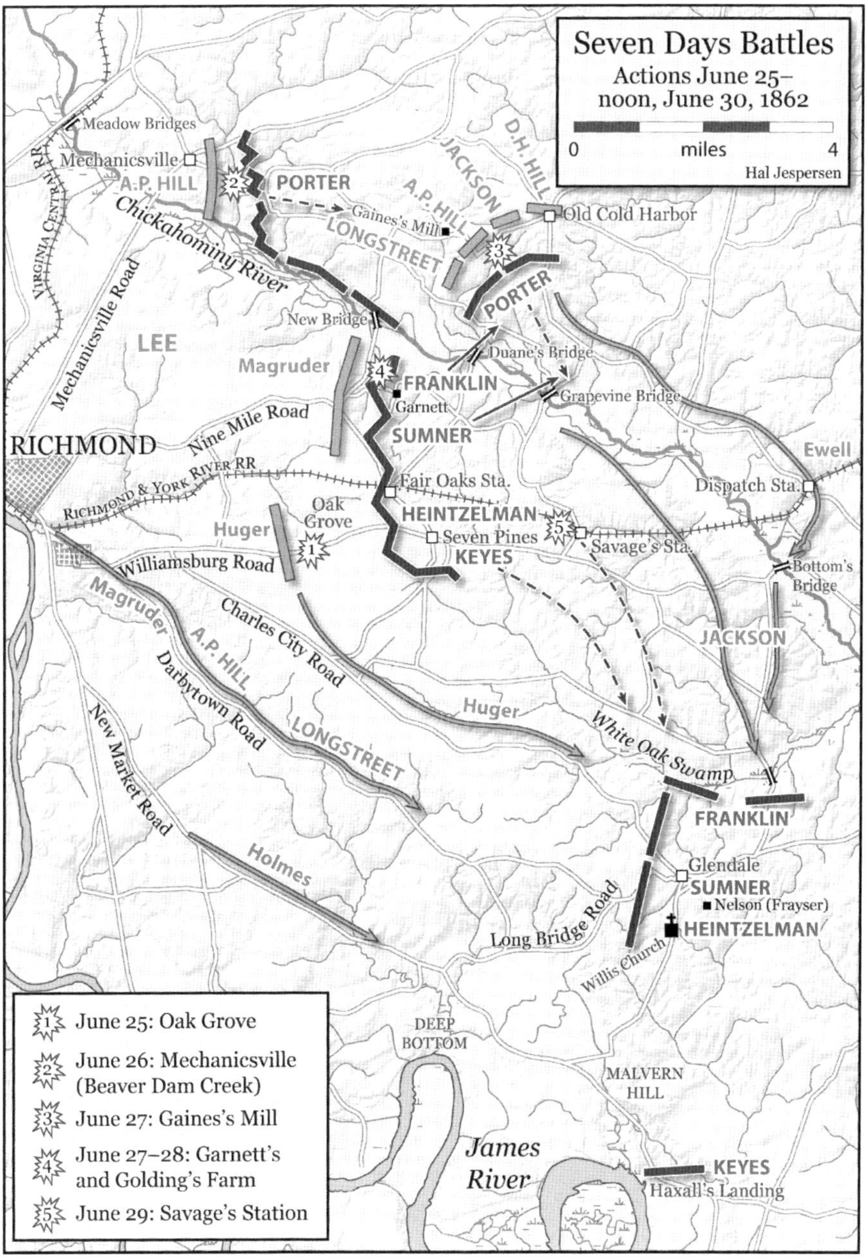

"Seven Days Battles." *Map by Hal Jespersen.*

forcing them out of their defenses, the Confederates attacked their strong position head-on, and their assault at Beaver Dam Creek was met with a bloody repulse. Why Jackson did not attack has been the subject of debate since the battle. In his official report, Jackson made no mention of an order from Lee to attack that day but did state that he "distinctly heard the rapid and continuous discharges of cannon."[4]

Although victorious on the field, McClellan knew that Jackson was in the area, and if the Confederate should fall on Porter's right flank, it could threaten his supply base and lead to disaster. McClellan directed Porter to hold a position north of the Chickahominy for another day in order to give the army a chance to begin to move its supply base from White House Landing south to the James River. With his corps, Porter selected a very strong position behind Boatswain's Creek. The Confederates followed and launched a series of attacks that lasted through the afternoon but met with no success. After suffering a major delay by being led down the wrong road, Jackson's men arrived on the army's left flank late in the afternoon. Near dusk, Lee ordered one final assault. After being shifted to the right, the Texas Brigade under John Bell Hood broke through, and on the left, other men of Jackson's command did the same. The Union position collapsed, but the Fifth Corps was saved by nightfall and retreated across the river. Having narrowly escaped disaster, McClellan's force began its slow movement to the James River, where it would set up its new supply base.

Gaines's Mill had been the second-bloodiest day of the war thus far (only Shiloh exceeded it in violence). The Federals had roughly 31,000 men in the fight and lost 6,837. George McCall's division of the Fifth Corps had suffered more than 200 casualties at Mechanicsville and about 1,600 at Gaines's Mill. The Confederates took about 57,000 men north of the Chickahominy and lost roughly 8,000. Lee could not afford many days such as this. He had driven Porter across the Chickahominy, but the Federal army still threatened the Confederate capital. Displaying the cautious style that would mark his career, McClellan did not attack but began moving his army to the James, where it would be under the protection of the Federal gunboats. While Lee had saved Richmond for the moment, his opponent was slipping away. He knew that the Confederacy had limited resources in comparison to the Union, and its best chance of winning independence would be in an early victory. A prolonged war would work against it. With a great opportunity before him, how could Lee bring McClellan to bay before he escaped?[5]

Chapter 2

The Opponents

The armies that were preparing to face each other near Glendale (Frayser's Farm) were quite different from each other. In fact, they were each very unlike what they had been the previous July at the battle at Manassas. George McClellan had taken the defeated mob that had retreated to Washington and had re-formed it into a huge and what appeared to be effective fighting machine. McClellan was a young and brash commander. A graduate of West Point and former railroad executive, he was only thirty-four years old when he took command of the nation's most prominent army. The fate of the nation seemed to be in his hands. Seemingly confident to the highest degree, he and his army gave the impression that they were prepared for great things.

Unfortunately for the Lincoln administration, McClellan was not all he appeared to be. While he was outstanding at the tasks involved in building an army, those skills did not translate into effective combat leadership. As is so often the case, McClellan's greatest strengths were also his greatest weaknesses. Having built a magnificent machine, he was afraid to let it suffer damage. He had been an observer during the Crimean War and had seen the carnage possible in modern warfare. To his credit, McClellan was not extravagant with his men's lives. He was not aggressive but rather preferred to pin the enemy down, bring up his artillery and defeat the enemy while incurring minimal risks. These were seemingly noble qualities in a commander, but when combined with several other tendencies, they spelled disaster for the Army of the Potomac and for the men he sought to protect. McClellan was not at all as self-confident as he seemed to be. When confronted with an enemy, he tended to overrate its size and capabilities, resulting in almost self-paralysis. He sought to preserve his force and avoid destruction rather than use its power to crush his foe. Although McClellan's traits were not a problem when he was faced with an equally cautious opponent, when an aggressive enemy was in his front, they became quite evident.

The Army of the Potomac was not the fighting machine that it would become later in the war. It was organized into five corps, each of which typically contained two divisions (the Fifth Corps consisted of three). Generally, each division contained three brigades. This provided the army commander a more efficient span of control, as it would be an almost impossible task for the commander to provide effective command and control of all the independent divisions during a battle. Each of the corps was assigned a section of cavalry. This would be useful in serving as scouts and in screening the corps from the enemy, but only a small force made up the army reserve. The dispersion of the cavalry among the corps would prove to be disastrous when faced with their highly effective Southern counterparts.

Artillery was also divided, and it was split among the divisions and the corps, with a central reserve commanded by the very capable Colonel Henry Hunt, who learned very quickly that artillery was more effective when it was massed. By the following year, then general Hunt would have centralized a great deal of artillery into very powerful force that he would use with great effectiveness.

The corps commanders were an undistinguished lot, not at all up to the future standards of the Army of the Potomac. Edwin V. Sumner was sixty-five, the oldest major general in the Federal army. He was nicknamed "Bull Head," allegedly because an enemy ball had bounced off his head during the Mexican-American War. While he was aggressive, he would not be an effective corps leader. William B. Franklin was thirty-nine and was an experienced and effective administrator, but his abilities in the field did little to inspire confidence from those above or below him. Fitz John Porter was a favorite of McClellan's. He had put up a solid defense at both Beaver Dam Creek and Gaines's Mill and would do so again at Malvern Hill. Unfortunately for Porter, he would run afoul of John Pope in August at Second Manassas, and his active command would come to an end.[6]

Although the talent at the level of corps command left much to be desired, the leaders of some of the divisions and brigades showed a great deal of promise and would become the future leaders of the army. Among them were division commanders such as John Sedgwick, who would rise to command of the Sixth Corps. Israel Richardson would be effective, but his career would be cut short in the fields of Antietam. Phil Kearny, a dynamic leader, might have risen to army command but instead was killed in September at Chantilly. Henry Slocum would become a corps commander. Joseph Hooker would be promoted to army command the following winter and would meet with disaster at Chancellorsville. Later, he would be transferred to the Western Theater, where he enjoyed more success. At the brigade level was John Reynolds, who would be very capable but would meet his fate as the commander of the First Corps the next July 1 at Gettysburg. Winfield Scott Hancock would lead the Second Corps at Gettysburg and arguably became one of the army's finest corps commanders. Henry Hunt would rise to the command of the Federal artillery, where he would demonstrate a high level of effectiveness. George Meade would, of course, rise to the command of the Army of the Potomac just a few days before Gettysburg.

The Confederate army was quite a different lot. It was led by Robert E. Lee, who would be an audacious commander, perhaps one of the finest in American military history. He commanded a force of separate divisions (the Confederate government had not yet authorized the creation of a corps-level structure). This would be problematic for Lee, as it caused a very wide stretch of direct supervision. At this point of the war, Confederate high command had a distinct advantage in quality over its Federal counterpart. The most famous at the time was Thomas "Stonewall" Jackson, who, together with Lee, had masterminded the strategy for dealing with the Union forces in the Shenandoah Valley and then took their plan and executed the brilliant campaign that drove the enemy troops from the Valley. Under Jackson's command was the solid division commander Richard Ewell, who would later rise to corps command.

D.H. Hill was a division leader, competent and aggressive, but his personality would lead to future difficulties with Lee. James Longstreet would, after Jackson's death at Chancellorsville the next spring, rise to become Lee's most trusted subordinate. A very capable leader, Longstreet displayed some disturbing traits, such as unfairly deflecting the blame for the failure of the Seven Pines attack to Benjamin Huger. A.P. Hill was an aggressive but often impetuous field commander and would rise to command of the Third Corps the next year. At the brigade level, John Bell Hood did a very solid job and was one of leaders who broke the Federal defenses at Gaines's Mill. Other competent commanders included Micah Jenkins, Charles Field, Lafayette McLaws, Jubal Early, Joseph Kershaw, Lewis Armistead and Cadmus Wilcox. The cavalry was centralized and was led by J.E.B. Stuart, one of the war's finest cavalry leaders.

While the Confederate army was well stocked with talented leadership, all was not perfect. Lee would find three of the division commanders wanting, and they would be transferred out of the army soon after the current campaign. Benjamin Huger and Theophilus Holmes were thought to be not aggressive enough, and John Magruder had lost Lee's confidence because he could not seem to keep his emotions under control. Lee found that to be a serious flaw in a commander.

The artillery was dispersed, with a central reserve. Unfortunately, it was led by the unimaginative William Pendleton, who was not up to the task. An additional deficiency affected the artillery: it was well behind its counterpart in terms of the quality of its guns and ordnance. The Federal batteries were generally made up of six guns, as opposed to the Confederates' four. Almost all of the Union guns were the rifled Parrotts and Ordnance rifles, plus the effective twelve-pound Napoleons. Their counterparts had a variety of guns, including obsolete howitzers and six-pound smoothbores. The Federals enjoyed a decided advantage in weight, distance and supply. The Confederate guns often had a shorter range, and the six-pounders were completely outclassed. Additionally, the gun types were mixed in the Confederate batteries, causing major challenges for their supply officers. The quality of Confederate ordnance was also problematic. Porter Alexander wrote that the "smooth bore shells & shrapnel would frequently explode prematurely, & our rifled shot and shell…had no range at all." Fuses were unreliable. Fortunately for the Confederate army, many, but not all, of these problems would be remedied by the following spring.[7]

Chapter 3

MEETING AT THE STATION

It was the morning of June 28, 1862, and Robert E. Lee had a difficult decision to make. The Federal army had retreated across the Chickahominy, and now the entire Federal force was south of the river. What would McClellan do next? He seemed to have multiple choices. The most threatening was that McClellan could take his entire army and drive toward Richmond. Most of the Confederate force was north of the river, and although he had gained control of the New Bridge, Lee would need to repair others to more rapidly transfer his force across the river. Could that be done in time to stop a Union drive? Alternatively, McClellan could try to re-cross the Chickahominy to protect his supply base. He might retrace his steps back down the Virginia Peninsula, reorganize and move on Richmond again. Finally, McClellan could be moving to the James River. Lee had to be careful; if he guessed incorrectly, it could lead to disaster. Added to his concerns was the exhausted state of most of his army, parts of which had fought vicious engagements on the previous two days.

Lee didn't think that McClellan was likely to choose the first option. The Federal commander had not demonstrated much aggressiveness so far, and Lee thought it would be doubtful that so cautious a commander would strike toward Richmond with his supply base exposed to the Confederates. He believed it entirely conceivable that the Federal commander might re-cross the Chickahominy and fight for his White House Landing base. The last two choices were also very possible. In order to ascertain whether McClellan planned to move down the Peninsula, Lee sent Richard Ewell's division and the 9th Virginia Cavalry to seize the York River railroad and ordered Stuart and his cavalry to Dispatch Station. "Columns of dust south of the Chickahominy" soon told Lee that the Federals were in motion. Stuart reported that the enemy had burned the railroad bridge over the Chickahominy, which meant that McClellan would not move in that direction. He might, however, move to the lower bridges over that river and still head east. Lee thought it "necessary that our troops should continue on the north bank of the river," and until McClellan's true intentions were determined, Ewell was ordered to proceed to Bottom's Bridge. The cavalry was to watch the bridges below. South of the river, the Federal works opposite Benjamin Huger and John B. Magruder were fully manned, with the area below them being "densely wooded and intersected by impassable swamps." With Huger and Magruder being unable to divine McClellan's intentions, they "were therefore compelled to wait until his purpose should be developed." By late afternoon and early evening, it was becoming clear to Lee. His pickets had not discovered any indication of a Federal move toward the lower Chickahominy bridges. McClellan was heading for the James.[8]

The Federal commander had limited options in moving his army south. It would have few north–south roads on which to travel, the most notable being the road across White Oak Swamp. The army would not be able to move quickly, as his progress would be limited by the slow speed of his supply trains. McClellan had roughly 100,000 men, 281 field guns, 26 pieces of heavy siege artillery, 3,800 wagons and ambulances and a herd of 2,500 beef. It would take time to move such a large army. To compound the problem, the bridge over White Oak Swamp had been heavily damaged, and it was not until two hours after daylight on the twenty-eighth that it was usable. By that evening, another bridge, two miles to the west at Brackett's Ford, was also ready.[9]

Lee, on the other hand, had a good road network with which to work. Four roads ran roughly west–east. The northernmost was the Williamsburg Road, followed by Charles City, Darbytown and New Market Roads. Darbytown eventually ran into another road called Long Bridge. An interesting thing was that the White Oak, Charles City and Long Bridge roads all converged at an intersection near Riddell's Shop (now known as Glendale). The New Market Road ran parallel to the James River, but it split just before Malvern Hill; the northern branch was Long Bridge Road. For McClellan, it was crucial that he keep the road junction open. Another potentially important spot was just south of that intersection. Malvern Hill was a gently rising slope, perfect for artillery, and could command a movement toward the

James. If McClellan could get there first and hold it, his progress would be much more secure.[10]

The Riddell's Shop intersection was therefore critical to Lee. If he could get his army there before McClellan, he would have an opportunity to severely damage or destroy his opponent. If he could get his own artillery on Malvern Hill and block McClellan's retreat, so much the better. The trick for Lee was how to get to the crossroads first. McClellan held one advantage: he had slipped out of his works on the twenty-eighth and was heading south, leaving a very strong force to protect his rear. Most of the Confederate army was still north of the Chickahominy River, and few bridges were in good enough shape to get the army across rapidly.

Lee needed to buy time, and he had several options. The command of John B. Magruder (which included his division and those of Lafayette McLaws and David R. Jones) and the division of Benjamin Huger were already south of the river, so they could be moved to Glendale. However, until adequate Confederate forces could cross the Chickahominy, Richmond would be exposed to a direct Federal attack. As unlikely as that might have seemed to Lee, he could not afford to take that chance. He decided that he would use Huger and Magruder to threaten and slow the Federal retreat. A.P. Hill and Longstreet would cross the Chickahominy at New Bridge, move down Darbytown Road and then march up Long Bridge Road to Glendale. Jackson would repair the bridges over the Chickahominy in his sector and could then perform several functions: guard against a Federal re-crossing, be in a good position should McClellan move east and be able to harass McClellan's rear should the Federals move toward the James. Theophilus Holmes could be brought up from Petersburg, moved down the New Market Road and possibly seize Malvern Hill. If that eminence could be secured, McClellan would effectively be in a Confederate vise. Holmes would block his way to the river. A.P. Hill and Longstreet would hammer him at Glendale, to be joined by Huger and Magruder. Jackson could attack his rear. It was a recipe for disaster for the Federals, but everything depended on swift movement and good timing by the Confederates. As audacious and challenging as the plan might be, the potential reward was spectacular. Could they move quickly enough?

On the morning of the twenty-ninth, Colonel Lawrence Baker was ordered to take his 1st North Carolina Cavalry and ride down to the river (New Market) road to reconnoiter. Joined by the 3rd Virginia Cavalry, Baker took five companies of his regiment and proceeded to the junction of the Long Bridge and Charles City crossroads. Rumor had it that there was a

Federal camp near the church on the Willis Church Road (sometimes referred to as the "Quaker" road), and Baker wanted to see if that information was accurate. Near the crossroads, Baker encountered units of Averell's Union cavalry, who were posted in front of Couch's division. He "determined to drive back their cavalry force, which was covering their movements, and proceed to the Quaker Road." Averell's cavalry gave way "judiciously" until they were within fifty yards of the Federal artillery. Lieutenant Munk of the 1st Pennsylvania Artillery then opened with a section (two guns), firing canister and case shot, blasting the Confederate troopers. Baker's men suffered about eighty casualties and withdrew, but they had found out that the Federals were on the Willis Church road in force. Tom Rosser's cavalry, on Baker's right, confirmed the Union movement. If Lee harbored any more doubts about McClellan's intentions, they were now dispelled. The Federals were definitely heading for the river.[11]

Lee set his army in motion. A.P. Hill and Longstreet were ordered to cross the Chickahominy at New Bridge and head for the Darbytown and then the Long Bridge Roads. Huger and Magruder were directed to attack the Federals and slow their retreat. Magruder was to move down the Williamsburg Road, and Huger was to use the Charles City Road. As Huger and Magruder advanced, they found the Federal works abandoned, with "large quantities of military stores of every description abandoned or destroyed." Jackson was to cross at the Grapevine Bridge and "move down the south side of the Chickahominy." Lee said that this would lead Jackson to the "flank and rear of Savage's Station." However, before he could do anything, Jackson would have to reconstruct Grapevine Bridge and the more structurally sound Alexander's bridge nearby.[12]

Magruder, who had not slept that night, caught up with Lee on Nine Mile Road. As they discussed the plan, Magruder came to the misunderstanding that Huger would move down the Williamsburg Road, but in reality, the latter's division would actually be several miles away, on Charles City Road. He and Lee continued on to Fair Oaks Station, which had been abandoned by the Federals. Magruder said that Lee repeated his instructions and then rode off. Magruder continued in his pursuit of the Federals. As his men advanced, they could soon see black clouds of smoke rising from the vicinity of Savage's Station. The Union army was destroying everything it couldn't carry away. Mountains of beef, pork, hardtack, coffee, whiskey, medicine and rifles were in flames. An ammunition train was set ablaze and sent into the Chickahominy. Anything not necessary for the "safety or maintenance of the troops" was to be destroyed. Hospital patients who could move were

Samuel Heintzelman. *Courtesy of the Library of Congress.*

marched away; those who could not walk, plus their attendant physicians, would have to be left behind to the mercy of the Confederates. Those who remained healthy were now exhausted. They had "marched night and day… no sleep, scant food, and tired almost to death." The Federal commander was sacrificing all in the name of speed.[13]

McClellan ordered Porter's heavily bloodied Fifth Corps to cross White Oak Swamp and set up a position to cover the roads leading from Richmond toward the line of retreat. Erasmus D. Keyes was to take the Fourth Corps across the swamp to protect the movement of the Federal trains. The corps of Sumner, Franklin and Samuel P. Heintzelman, as well as William F. Smith's division, were to set up near Savage's Station to cover the rear of the movement. McClellan departed and crossed over White Oak Swamp, and unfortunately for the Federal soldiers, he left no one in charge.[14]

Magruder advanced, fully expecting that Huger would be on his right, on the Williamsburg Road, and that Jackson would cross the Grapevine Bridge. He estimated that thirty-five to forty thousand Confederates would strike the Federals both in the front and on the flanks. Joseph Kershaw's men went forward with skirmishers in front, and they soon found heavy obstructions on the railroad track. Clearing them, they soon made contact with the defenders, who were in "works well manned"; according to prisoners and to his scouts, the Federals had at least a division on hand. Magruder dispatched a staff officer to contact Jackson, and that officer returned stating that Jackson would need two hours to repair the damaged bridge. Adding to his growing consternation, Magruder received a message from Huger that the bulk of his force was not on the Williamsburg Road as anticipated. Instead of having the large number of troops he expected, Magruder was left to attack an unknown force with only his command. Nonetheless, on Sunday morning, June 29, Magruder followed instructions, and his men advanced.[15]

With no one left in charge, each Federal corps commander did what he thought was right. Sumner's Second Corps set up at Allen's farm, near the railroad, two miles from Savage's Station. Unfortunately, Sumner was out in front of Heintzelman and Franklin, so the lines were not contiguous and they could not support one another. The two Federal commanders were anxious for Sumner to fall back and help them to establish a solid defensive line. It was too late, however, and at 9:00 a.m. Magruder's advancing troops ran into Sumner. The fight lasted about two hours, but casualties were minimal, with the exception of Confederate general Richard Griffith, who was killed by a shell fragment while commanding a Mississippi brigade held in reserve.[16]

With his concern growing, Franklin rode to Allen's Farm and persuaded Sumner to pull back, which he did, and the Federals set up a strong defensive position at a railway depot named Savage's Station. On the north side of the railroad, behind the lines, there was a cleared field "filled with hospital tents laid out in rows." Inside each tent were fifteen or twenty men, on "comfortable clean beds, with the necessary surgeons and attendants." To the south, between the railroad and Williamsburg Road, was a clearing, nearly a half mile square, fronted by a ravine filled with undergrowth. To the east of the ravine were some small hills, good for defensive positions. To the west of the clearing was a stand of woods, where Franklin expected Heintzelman to be posted. South of Williamsburg Road were woods. Sumner's corps was stationed between the railroad and Williamsburg Road, with Burns's brigade of John Sedgwick's division in front. Sedgwick's remaining two

Edwin V. Sumner. *Courtesy of the Library of Congress.*

brigades were behind Burns. Israel Richardson's division was to the rear and slightly to the right. Baldy Smith was stationed in the woods to the left of Williamsburg Road. Near the front of the ravine and to the left, there were three batteries of artillery: Hazzard's, Pettit's and Osborn's. The corps of Franklin and Heintzelman were expected to be nearby, giving the Federals two corps plus Smith's division of the Sixth Corps to defend the rear of the Union retreat.[17]

When he arrived west of the station around noon, Magruder was aware that he still only had his own divisions on hand and requested that Lee send reinforcements. Huger was ordered to send two brigades down the Williamsburg Road and join Magruder's right. Apparently concerned that he might be attacked, and waiting for Jackson to cross the river, Magruder hesitated for several hours. This delay cost him the use

William B. Franklin. *Courtesy of the Library of Congress.*

of Huger's brigades, which were recalled at 2:00 p.m. Lee sensed that the troops facing Magruder were the Federal rear guard and that Huger's troops could be of better use elsewhere.[18]

Magruder was still hoping for Jackson to appear on his left, flanking the Federal defenders, but there was no sign of him. Time was wasting as he received a note indicating that Jackson could not cooperate, as he had "other important duty" to perform. Jackson did not clarify what that duty was. In any case, Major Walter Taylor, General Lee's aide, soon arrived and said that Jackson had been ordered to cooperate with Magruder and that he was unaware of any conflicting orders. Taylor wanted to speak with Jackson but did not know the way, so Reverend L.W. Allen, of Magruder's staff, was sent to find him. Jackson did not arrive until 3:30 a.m. the following morning. Without Huger and Jackson, Magruder now had only his own command on hand. Instead of the thirty-five to forty thousand men expected to participate in the battle, there were thirteen thousand. Nonetheless, his orders remained. He was to attack.[19]

At about 3:00 p.m., Confederate general Lafayette McLaws's command approached the station. Initially, he ordered Joseph Kershaw to send forward a regiment to "ascertain the conditions of things in the front," but Kershaw soon was directed to advance his South Carolinians (2nd, 3rd, 7th and 8th) along the tracks. Captain Del Kemper's battery was placed along the Williamsburg Road. Kershaw had been informed that Jackson should be coming down on his left, so he was to exercise caution should he see troops advancing. After about a mile, the South Carolinians began receiving artillery fire on their left flank. Fearing that it might be Jackson's men, Kershaw "restrained the fire of my men and sent a regimental battle-flag to the front to be waived on the railroad." It quickly became apparent that the fire was not from Jackson; it was from the Federals![20]

Union general William B. Franklin recalled the initial encounter:

> *Shortly before 4 o'clock General Sedgwick and I rode over to the hospital to visit some of our wounded friends…as we rode over an open field we saw a group of men come out of a wood on the north of the railroad, but some distance from the place where we expected to find Heintzelman. I thought they were our men, but General Sedgwick looked at them more closely, stopped, and exclaimed: "Why, those men are rebels!" We then turned back in as dignified a manner as circumstances would permit. But we had hardly started when they opened on us with a field-piece, keeping up a lively and uncomfortable fire.*[21]

At about 3:00 p.m., Kershaw received orders for his South Carolinians to advance, and he saw the enemy "occupying a series of heavy earthworks at the far end of the field on the Williamsburg Road." He halted his command at the brow of a hill and sent for Del Kemper's battery. The 2nd and 3rd South Carolina regiments were ordered to move along a ravine and flank the Federals. Kemper's guns arrived and fired with "rapidity and effect," dispersing the enemy infantry to the immediate front. Kershaw again ordered an advance, although he was concerned that there were no troops to protect his right and that he was exposed to a flank attack. Quickly he learned that McLaws was reinforcing his right, having ordered Semmes's brigade south of the road. Kershaw's men advanced over the rising ground. Magruder ordered Kershaw to continue to advance, and another "heavy force" of enemy troops was encountered. Del Kemper's guns were placed on the road, with Henagan's 8th South Carolina on the right, across the road. The 7th South Carolina was also ordered forward. The colonel of the 7th South Carolina, D. Wyatt Aiken, at first ordered his troops to hold their fire but soon directed them to "load advancing and fire at will." They were driving the enemy before them, through the woods into the adjacent field, "throwing them into confusion and strewing the ground with dead." Soon, Federal troops appeared on the right, threatening Kershaw's flank. Kemper's battery continued to fire and "inflicted terrible havoc upon the enemy, whose dead lay in heaps along the road, scarcely 200 yards from the battery."[22]

Union general William Burns remembered Kershaw's attack: "[T]he dispositions were in progress when the enemy attacked furiously

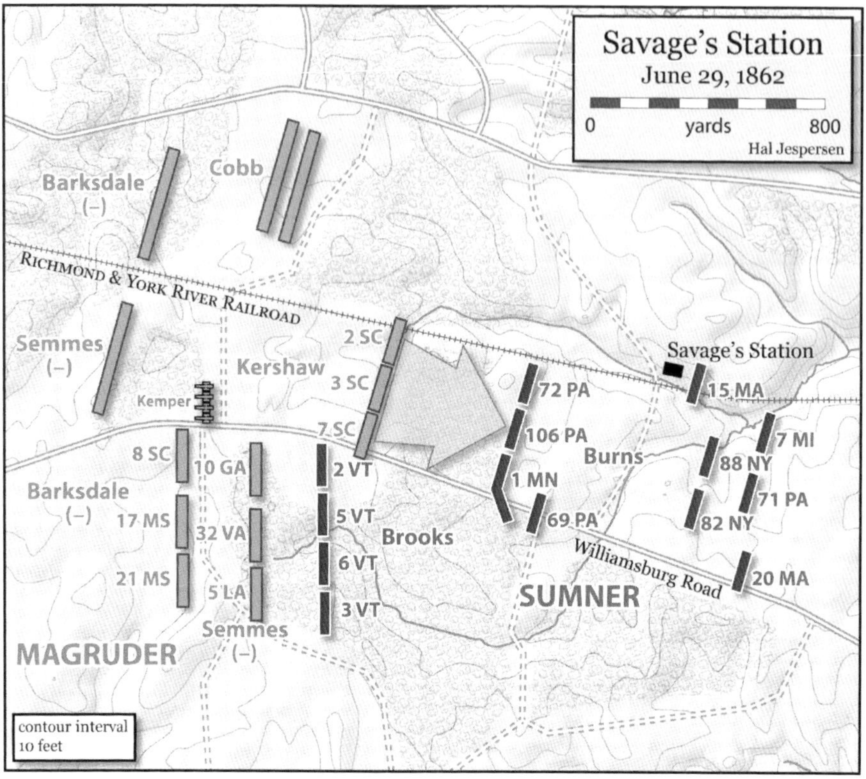

Savage's Station. *Map by Hal Jespersen.*

with infantry, he having been playing with artillery upon me." Burns had been ordered by Sumner to take two regiments and hold the woods that lay between the railroad and the Williamsburg Road, and he positioned the 72nd and 106th Pennsylvania. As Kershaw advanced, the fight gravitated toward Burns's position. Not having enough troops to cover his position, he sent word to Sumner for support. The 1st Minnesota arrived and was promptly placed on his left. Burns needed yet more men to cover his line, as his center was dangerously thin. More regiments were sent in support, but before they arrived, the Confederates made a rush for the middle and Burns was wounded. For a moment, the attackers broke through, but Burns's "brave men rallied and drove them back." The 88th New York "came across the field double-quicking and cheering." Burns positioned at the Williamsburg Road, just as the fight shifted there. "The enemy opened artillery and infantry on them, but they never faltered." Soon the 82nd New York arrived, and it was placed in the center, followed by the 69th Pennsylvania Volunteers, which was placed to the left of the 1st Minnesota. The 15th Massachusetts and the 20th Massachusetts came up, joined by the 1st California and the 7th Michigan. These last two units were held in reserve.[23]

Confederate general Lafayette McLaws sent Paul Semmes's brigade below the Williamsburg Road in order to support Kershaw. Semmes advanced the 10th Georgia and the 32nd Virginia and then the 5th Louisiana. As they advanced through thick woods, they made out some troops about forty yards in front of them. These were the men of William Brooks's brigade of Smith's division. In the thick underbrush, Semmes ordered Private Maddox of the 5th Louisiana to challenge, "Who are you?" The reply came back: "Friends." Semmes heard the reply and demanded, "What regiment?" The response was quick: "Third Vermont!" The Confederates immediately commenced firing, and the action continued until darkness overtook the field.[24]

William Brooks, commander of Smith's Second Brigade, had earlier passed Savage's Station on his way to the White Oak Bridge. When the Confederate presence was discovered, he was ordered to return to the field

Savage's Station. *Courtesy of the Library of Congress.*

and was placed on the left of Williamsburg Road. In the woods, he positioned the 5th and 6th Vermont regiments in front, with the 2nd and 3rd behind them in reserve. As soon as the firing began, the two reserve regiments were deployed, and they opened on the enemy. The firing was intense, with some of the Vermonters using all of the sixty rounds of ammunition allotted to them. Lieutenant Colonel Lewis Grant was leading the 5th and "ordered a bayonet charge, which was executed at a double-quick in splendid style." The Confederate force there broke. Wounded in the leg, Brooks remained with his troops and his regiments halted the Confederate advance, but a "galling fire" continued until nightfall.[25]

The fight between Semmes and Brooks occurred to the right rear of Kershaw's attack. South of the road, John Henegan's 8th South Carolina (under Kershaw) was ordered to halt around 6:00 p.m. He spent some time moving his men, dodging Federal artillery, and then received orders to advance. Semmes's 10th Georgia passed over his line in the woods to his front. Moving his men to get clear of the 10th, he received fire from both his front and from Semmes's troops in his rear. Henegan ordered his men to lie down in order to avoid the crossfire. Other units had difficulty with the terrain. In the thick woods, Colonel Wyatt Aiken of the 7th South Carolina heard firing to his rear but could not make out the source. He sent a sergeant major to assess the situation, and he returned to state that the enemy was in his rear. Aiken responded by pulling back his men about fifty yards.[26]

Magruder ordered two of William Barksdale's regiments, the 17th and 21st Mississippi, up in support of the attack. They advanced "gallantly and promptly" and fired several volleys. They were soon asked to cease firing, for fear of the "danger [that] would result from it to our friends." Darkness was falling on the battlefield.[27]

Sumner had learned that he did not actually have three corps on hand but two. Although McClellan had left no one in charge, Sumner was the ranking general, and he had ordered Heintzelman to set up his troops for defense. As no one was technically in command, Heintzelman ordered his troops to pull out and head for the White Oak crossings. In defense of his decision, Heintzelman later wrote, "[T]he whole open space near Savage's was crowded with troops-more than I supposed could be brought in action judiciously." He also thought it "impossible for all the troops to retire by the roads leading by Savage Station." It was just too many men and too much equipment to move quickly. As a consequence of McClellan's absence, a large part of the Federal defensive force had melted away. Sumner was furious.[28]

Although tactically a draw, the action at Savage's Station was strategically successful for the Federals, as it held the attackers at bay and bought precious time for McClellan's army to continue to move south. For the Confederates, it was an exercise in frustration. What could have been a powerful assault of up to forty thousand men on the Union rear devolved into a struggle between a few brigades. Jackson's hammer blow failed to materialize. Huger never appeared on the Confederate right, and Magruder was left to attack with only his division. Lee was extremely disappointed. He knew that an opportunity had been lost to strike a blow at McClellan and set him up for even a larger one that could possibly destroy the Federal army. Would he ever have such a chance again? That evening, Lee wrote to Magruder:

> *I regret much that you have made so little progress today in the pursuit of the enemy. In order to reap the fruits of our victory the pursuit should be more vigorous. I urge you, then, again to press on his rear rapidly and steadily. We must lose no more time or he will escape us entirely…. P.S. Since the above was written I learn from Major Taylor that you are under the impression that General Jackson has been ordered not to support you. On the contrary, he has been directed to do so, and to push the pursuit vigorously.*[29]

Lee's rebuke does not seem to be entirely justified. Magruder had not been as aggressive as Lee would have liked, but he was exhausted and under medication. He committed only nine of his twenty-eight available regiments (3,100 of 13,000 men) to the battle and has received criticism from historians for this. In his defense, Magruder sensed that his command faced at least a corps of Federals, and this was borne out the next morning when he learned that his men had captured prisoners from three Union divisions. In fact, he faced two corps; he was outnumbered with no support. To attack with more troops likely would have resulted only in the sacrifice of more men. It was a very difficult situation. Lee expected Magruder to pin down the rear Union corps. A more forceful attack might have done that, but at great cost. The blame for the Confederate failure at the station does not appear to fall at Magruder's feet alone. Jackson and Huger certainly share the responsibility, as does Lee's staff work. It must be remembered that this was a new army, and this was its first campaign. When Jackson did not appear and Huger did not coordinate, Lee should have been kept apprised and should have sent staff to ensure that his plans were carried out. This problem had appeared a few days earlier in the campaign and would show its head again before the week was out.[30]

"Savage Station" by Henry Clow. *Courtesy of the County of Henrico, Virginia Historical Preservation and Museum Services.*

The day had been costly enough, considering that the only benefit went to the Federals, who succeeded in buying much-needed time. The Confederate losses have been estimated at 375 and the Federal at 600, plus the approximately 2,500 to 3,000 sick and wounded who would be left behind to the Confederates. Numbers are deceiving. While this battle was small in scope, it was desperate to those engaged, and the individual suffering was the same as in more famous engagements. A report in the *Charleston Daily Courier* provides the evidence:[31]

> *I beheld another sight, which few, thank God, have ever witnessed. In the middle of the yard something was lying upon the ground. At first glance I supposed it to be a roll of dirty blankets, but observing that it had motion, I walked up to it…A faint voice ejaculated, "Water!" I could hardly believe my senses. There lay a man, with the right side of his face, including the eye, nose, right ear and the entire right lobe of the brain shot away…maggots, mosquitoes, ticks, flies and vermin of every description filling the hole by the millions….a mass of corruption, suffering the torments of the damned and yet unable to die.*[32]

A Confederate soldier, Robert Boyd of the 7th South Carolina, wrote to his father:

> *How we hav com throw Safe I cannot tell for the Bulet and canon Ball cum all around me as thick as iver I saw hale fall…. we hav gand a grat victory we hav driv the scondrels Back…i am in grat hops that the war wil come to and en be for long I don't think it will last much longer for we whip them in ouer fight.*

Boyd went on to describe what the Yankees had left behind:

> [F]*ine guns the infield Rifle and we got coffee anuf to do us severl days* [??] *Socks, blankits tens wagons Horses comsary stors and a great miney other things…*[As for the battlefield itself, he noted:] *A Sit it is to go on the battle feld after battle the men la so thick that you mit walk them out* [??] *of setting your foot on the grond O it is all a dreadful sit to her the morning of woned an to see men shoot doon all around you round you.*[33]

Questions were raised almost immediately and have continued to the present day: What happened to the mighty Stonewall? Why did he not attack on the Union northern flank? The leader of the spectacular Valley Campaign, Jackson had been largely ineffectual thus far on the outskirts of Richmond. Following Gaines's Mill, his men were on the north bank of the Chickahominy. He had two bridges to rebuild, Grapevine and Alexander's, one of which was three or four hundred yards above the other. The Federals had destroyed these during their withdrawal, and without them Jackson could not follow the retreating bluecoats. Curiously, he ordered Major Dabney, who was a preacher before the war and was not an experienced engineer, to rebuild the bridges. Not surprisingly, this was something that Dabney was unable to do. Jackson then sent for Captain C.R. Mason, who was an engineer but was some fifteen or sixteen miles away. When he finally arrived and began the work, Mason stated that given enough men for labor, he could complete the bridge in two hours, which he did. However, night would fall before the work would be complete. Time was slipping away.[34]

Some have argued that Jackson was near exhaustion. After fighting in the Valley, he traveled one hundred miles to Richmond to meet with Lee and then, without delay, returned to the Valley to gather his troops. Immediately, he pushed them to Richmond, giving him precious opportunity to rest. The distinguished and generally reliable Confederate artillerist Edward Porter Alexander was quite critical of Jackson and attributed his slow performance to other motives. Alexander stated that although the bridges would have to be rebuilt, Stonewall's troops could have crossed at a ford used on the old country road that led to the Grapevine Bridge. This, of course, was by no means certain. Jackson's command contained some twenty-five thousand men, plus artillery, supply wagons and the like. For all of his force to have efficiently crossed at one country ford seems implausible. Alexander also stated that the New Bridge was only three miles away, implying that Jackson could have traveled by that route. However, use of that bridge would have been problematic, as it was to be used by Longstreet and A.P. Hill. Alexander also suggested another reason for Jackson's slowness: "[T]his was Sunday, and Jackson gave it strict observance. The greater part of his troops remained in camp all day and until after midnight Sunday night." While Stonewall's strict dedication to his faith was well known, there is no proof that this was the reason for his performance.[35]

Jackson's biographer, Dr. James Robertson, argued that Jackson was obeying orders. A note signed by Lee's assistant adjutant, Colonel R.H. Chilton, stated that Jackson was to watch the Chickahominy and resist any Federal effort to cross. When General Jones of Magruder's command arrived and inquired as to when Jackson would come to Magruder's aid, he received the "other important duty to perform" response.[36]

D. Scott Hartwig has noted another challenge that faced Jackson's group: he kept details to himself when it might have been better to share them with his subordinates. His commanders were often unclear about his intentions. Jackson also demonstrated poor staff work. Delegation was not his strength, and his chief of staff was Robert Dabney, a minister whom Jackson admired. Dabney was not a good choice for the position. The result of these shortcomings was that Jackson's group depended on his direct supervision. When he was unable to perform, so were they.[37]

While the reasons for Jackson's tardy performance on the twenty-ninth continue to be debated, several things seem clear. He had received the note delivered by Colonel Chilton ordering him to stay north of the river. That alone would seem sufficient explanation, as Jackson was meticulous about obeying orders. Added to that was exhaustion and the need to repair two bridges. Poor staff work and communication played a significant role. Unfortunately for the Confederates, things would not get better the next day; in fact, they would get worse.

Chapter 4

Racing Against the Clock

Soon after the fighting at Savage's Station had ended, Franklin suggested to Sumner that they follow McClellan's directive and begin their march toward the river. Sumner immediately balked, exclaiming, "No, General, you shall not go, nor will I go—I never leave a victorious field. Why! if I had twenty thousand more men, I would crush this rebellion." Franklin said that he would show the order from McClellan. After some difficulty in locating a candle, Sumner read it and exclaimed, "General McClellan did not know the circumstances when he wrote that note." At his "wit's end," Franklin replied that McClellan had anticipated just such a fight, and unless he and Sumner began moving, they could put the entire movement in jeopardy. If they delayed, the Confederates could be on them "in force to defeat us utterly the next morning." The ever-cautious Franklin was justified in his concern. Jackson had not yet crossed the Chickahominy, but when he did, his large command would be coming down on the Union northern flank. In support of Franklin, General Smith presented his aide-de-camp, Lieutenant Mathew Berry, who said that he had seen McClellan shortly before and that the commander expected all of the troops to be across the swamp before morning. It was "with great reluctance" that Sumner agreed to proceed south.[38]

During the night, the Federal troops who had been north of the White Oak Swamp headed for the bridge. George Batchelder remembered, "The march this night was terribly wearing on the men, particularly the sick & wounded." As they marched, men dropped out and fell asleep by the roadside, only to be aroused by the cavalry bringing up the rear. The riders "would wake up every sleeper, and start them along with the unvarying story that the rebels were close on their rear." The men would march but soon fell out again, "with the certain prospect of being prisoners at daylight." Although many fell behind, most reached the bridge and crossed, with Israel Richardson's division bringing up the rear. His men began their march at about 1:00 a.m. on the morning of the thirtieth and marched "nearly until daybreak." When they reached the bridge, they came upon a mass of

Israel Richardson. *Courtesy of the Library of Congress.*

stragglers from other parts of the army, with men packed in so tightly that they were unable to move. Richardson, "swearing like a trooper," and his staff struggled to get them untangled and over the bridge. By 10:00 a.m., all had crossed over, and the bridge had been destroyed. The Federals also demolished the bridge at Brackett's Ford, about two miles to the west.[39]

Captain George Hazzard was in for a surprise: he and his battery were left behind. Exhausted, they had slept while the rest of the army packed up and headed for the river. The next morning, he heard reveille, but from a direction not occupied by his comrades the night before! Quickly realizing his predicament, Hazzard ordered his men to quietly move away, walking so as not to attract notice. When they had cleared the vicinity of the enemy, they began to pick up their pace, and they reached the bridge just as Israel Richardson's men were preparing to destroy it. As his men headed for the rest of the army, they came across many stragglers and gave them warning that the Confederates were right behind, thus saving many from capture. Franklin admired Hazzard's courage and actions but lamented that he was mortally wounded later that day.[40]

While his men continued to move toward the river, McClellan sought to protect his rear at the White Oak and Brackett's crossings, as well as at the vital crossroads at Glendale, and he did this without concern over unit cohesion. At the White Oak Bridge area, Richardson's Division of the Second Corps, Smith's Division of the Sixth Corps, Naglee's Brigade of the Fourth Corps and three artillery batteries were stationed to contest any attempted crossing. Their position was strong. On the north side of the swamp, from which the Confederates would be approaching, the road dropped down and passed through low, open ground for a quarter mile, which was "open to artillery from the south [Federal] side." To the Confederate right, however, there were hills covered with woods, providing good cover for enemy artillery. On the Federal side, the road rose from the bridge and extended about a mile and a quarter to Long Bridge Road, which ran about two miles to the Glendale crossroads. The swamp was fringed with trees, but there were some clearings at the top of the rise; a small farmhouse stood with some outbuildings. With the bridges at White Oak and Brackett's destroyed, the Confederates could still cross the swamp in spots, but the Federals would be able to contest any effort.[41]

A few miles away, McCall's battered division, exhausted after its actions at Beaver Dam Creek and Gaines's Mill, was posted across Long Bridge Road, one of the approaches to the Glendale crossroads. A portion of Slocum's men remained near Brackett's Ford. For the men of the Federal army, it had been a long and difficult night. "Men were exhausted with the excitement of battle, want of sleep and food." It had been nearly impossible to find water, and when they halted for a few moments, they found that "the wells were drained and the springs made muddy." Mostly they had hard bread and some coffee, but every so often they could hear the squealing of some unlucky pigs. The men continued on, knowing that failure to keep up with the rest of the army could mean disaster.[42]

Part of Porter's Fifth Corps, George W. Morell's and George Sykes's divisions, plus a portion of the reserve artillery, had been sent south of Glendale in order to select a position to protect the remainder of the army's withdrawal. Porter quickly recognized the natural strength of Malvern Hill, which commanded the roads leading from Richmond and the Chickahominy Swamp. He posted the artillery on the hill and ordered Warren's brigade to station itself across the River Road to protect the army's flank. While the Union position at Malvern Hill was very strong, the rest of the army remained in great peril. Amazingly, McClellan once again left his army without clear leadership or direction and headed for the river to meet with the navy.[43]

As frustrated as Lee was with the lack of success on the twenty-ninth, he still had an opportunity to inflict potentially catastrophic damage on his opponent. Jackson had recalled Ewell from his watch at Bottom's Bridge and was at full strength. Longstreet and A.P. Hill had crossed the Chickahominy at New Bridge and—after a long, hot, twelve-hour march—had spent the night camped on Darbytown Road at the farm of Jacob Atlee (modern-day Dorey Park). Huger's division had not accomplished much and spent the night on the Brightwell Farm on Charles City Road. Theophilus Holmes had crossed the James and was moving up the River Road, where Walker's Brigade joined him. Holmes's section had some 5,170 infantry, 130 cavalry troops and four batteries of artillery.[44]

Jackson began his movement on the thirtieth, with his men finally crossing the Chickahominy, and he arrived at Magruder's camp around 3:30 a.m. Greatly relieved to see Jackson, the exhausted Magruder finally grabbed an hour's sleep, his "first in forty-eight." At daylight, his men and Jackson's discovered the urgency of the Federal retreat. About 2,500 sick and wounded, plus medical staff, had been left behind. As many as 1,000 stragglers were taken prisoner, and Confederates who had previously been captured were set free. D.H. Hill came upon a terrible sight, "what seemed to be an entire regiment of Federals cold in death," and learned that the 5th Vermont had been slaughtered "in the desperate charge upon the division of McLaws" at Savage's Station[45]

Hospital at Savage's Station. *Courtesy of the Library of Congress.*

There was also an unimaginable abundance of supplies—some burned, but many still useable. These included mountains of grain, rice, beef, thousands of axes, shovels, an abundance of medicine, rifles, knapsacks and blankets. Henry Berkeley of the Hanover (Virginia) Artillery remembered it seeming that there were enough blankets and tents to supply 100,000 men. John Casler of the 33rd Virginia saw great piles of burned coffee, some of it still of use, and they went for it "heavy." There were "great stacks of bacon, crackers and desiccated vegetables…a revelation" to the hungry rebels. The 4th and 5th North Carolina were left behind to escort the prisoners and the haul of booty back to Richmond. As happy as the hungry Confederates were to see this bounty, not all sights were so well received: "There were other mementoes of their stay and of their hasty departure left by 'our friends the enemy,' not quite so attractive or appetizing—the ghastly leavings of numerous field hospitals; pale, naked corpses and grotesque piles of arms and legs."[46]

Lee's anxiety was growing; he could not let McClellan escape. With the lack of success the previous day, every moment now was crucial. Each hour saw the Union army slipping through his grasp. The Confederate commander well knew

Thomas J. "Stonewall" Jackson. *Courtesy of the Library of Congress.*

that a long war would be to the South's disadvantage and that he had to try and end it as quickly as possible. Before him was a golden opportunity to strike a major blow to the Union war effort. He rode to meet Jackson and discuss his plans in person. According to artillerist Robert Stiles, the commanding general was immaculately attired. He rode up and "gracefully dismounted." Jackson, on the other hand, "appeared worn down to the lowest point of flesh consistent with effective service." His clothes were "one neutral dust tint," and his cap "was pulled so low in front that the visor cut the glint of his eyeballs." Stiles remembered that the two generals "greeted each other warmly, but wasted no time upon the greeting." Jackson was facing Stiles, who was about thirty feet away, and he saw the Valley commander begin to talk in "a jerky, impetuous way" and draw "a diagram on the ground with the toe of his right boot." After scratching out two sides of a triangle, Jackson traced the third line "slowly and with hesitation, alternately looking up at Lee's face and down at his diagram." Stonewall talked "earnestly," and when he completed the triangle, "he raised his foot and stamped it down with emphasis, saying, 'we've got him.'" Jackson immediately called for his horse and quickly mounted it and rode away. After this discussion, it would seem that Lee and Jackson must have been on the same page, but as events unfolded, that does not seem to be certain.[47]

After speaking with Jackson, Lee visited Magruder and instructed him to take his command and move to Darbytown Road, where he was to provide a reserve for Longstreet and A.P. Hill. This Magruder did. His men marched twelve miles and arrived at Timberlake's Store, on the Darbytown Road, around 2:00 p.m. Soon after his arrival, Magruder received word from Lee to rest his troops but to be ready to move at any time.[48]

Chapter 5

Exercises in Futility

Benjamin Huger had a solid career in the old army but was not experienced in the field. He had commanded a number of arsenals and had been General Winfield Scott's chief of ordnance during the war in Mexico. He was assigned command of the Norfolk department in May 1861, his main achievement being the surrender of Norfolk to the advancing Union army and the burning of the *Virginia*. Following the ill-fated Confederate attack at Seven Pines, Huger was accused by Longstreet of poorly handling a division. He would add nothing to his reputation during the advance toward Glendale.[49]

On the twenty-ninth, while Magruder desperately needed support at Savage's Station, Huger had advanced down the Charles City Road, but he moved with great caution when what was really needed was speed. His brigades led by William Mahone and Lewis Armistead marched on the Charles City Road, while those of Robert Ransom (temporarily under Huger's command) and Ambrose Wright were sent to Magruder's aid. Huger received a message from Lee, instructing him to advance all of his troops down the road, and as nothing seemed to be happening on Magruder's front, he recalled Ransom and Wright. In his report, Lee stated that it was "apparent that the force in Magruder's front was covering the retreat of the main body." Apparently, Lee believed that Huger's troops could be put to better use attacking the Federal column in the Glendale area. Magruder was left to fend for himself.[50]

Huger was to continue to move down the Charles City Road, which led directly to the Glendale intersection. As he was the closest to the crossroads, he would strike first, and he would be on Longstreet and A.P. Hill's left flank, lending great weight to their attack. With Jackson's four divisions of 25,300 men coming down across White Oak Swamp on the Federals' northern flank, Longstreet and Hill's 19,200 and Huger's 12,000, plus Magruder's 13,000-man division in reserve, Lee would have a massive juggernaut, roughly 70,000 men, striking the front and right of the Federal defenders at Glendale. This would be one of Lee's greatest chances to deal the Union army a crushing blow. Everything would depend on timing and the initiative of each of Lee's subordinates. Theophilus Holmes was also to play a role. His men and artillery were to guard Lee's right flank on the river road and possibly harass the Union flank and supply trains if the opportunity presented itself.[51]

As Armistead and Mahone approached Brightwell's, the left flank came under fire from the other side of the swamp. A boy who had been across the swamp told Huger that Federals were on the other side, and Huger began to worry that the aggressive Union general Phil Kearny had not retreated down the road on the other side (the New Road) but instead might be on his flank and rear. Kearny, however, had been ordered to cross the swamp and move in the direction of Glendale. He left behind some marksmen of the 20th Indiana, along with some artillery, to slow down any possible pursuit by the Confederates. This probably accounts for the boy's story about the Federals still being in position. Afraid to move too quickly lest Kearny attack him from behind, Huger managed to progress only five miles down the road and stopped at Brightwell's for the night. Ransom and Wright caught up with the remainder of Huger's group.[52]

Benjamin Huger. *Courtesy of the Library of Congress.*

That night, Huger issued orders for Wright to move the Third Brigade out the following morning at daylight. They were to cross the swamp and head east down the New (Portugee) Road, protecting the division's left flank. Wright was to move toward the White Oak Bridge area, cautiously searching for the enemy. Soon his men captured two enemy pickets, who said that Kearny's men were moving away, heading toward the crossroads at Glendale. South of the swamp, Mahone's men were heading down the Charles City Road, with a scouting party out front. They soon returned, saying that the bluecoats were only a half mile away. Mahone placed his brigade in position to meet the potential threat and had a brush with the enemy's rear guard. They continued their advance as far as Fisher's Ford, where it was apparent that a large body of the enemy had been the evening before. As they approached Brackett's field, they finally ran into the rear guard of Kearny's men and found the road blocked by obstructions.[53]

Union general Slocum had ordered trees cut down to impede the Confederate movements. Rather than cut his way through the obstacles, Mahone, a former railroad construction engineer, made the fateful decision to cut a new road. As his men hacked their way, the Federals continued to chop down trees faster than the Confederates could advance. Rather than send a force ahead to simply stop the enemy from cutting, Mahone continued to chop away at a new road. After hacking away for about a mile, at Brackett's Field, he began to meet more serious resistance, and he became convinced that the enemy was "fortified by the advantages of a superior position." He decided to reconnoiter farther. Mahone placed a section of Moorman's Battery in position and opened fire, "which was returned with great energy and effect." Mahone was only two miles northwest of Glendale. The remainder of June 30 was basically spent in an artillery duel, with Mahone losing twenty-four killed and fifty-two wounded and the Union losing but twenty-five. By the time night had fallen, Huger had accomplished nothing. In his report, he said, "[W]e had many men killed and wounded." Amazingly, he made no mention of hearing the furious action only two miles away.[54]

Although Wright had made some progress across the swamp, the three brigades south of it managed to move forward only about a mile. The division that was to be the spearhead of the Confederate attack was frittering away the day with cautious movement and the attempted construction of a new road. It would stop only a few miles from the Glendale crossroads, within earshot of the storm that was to come, but it would offer precious little assistance. It is arguable that even after being joined by Wright, Huger did not have sufficient force to drive Slocum, but his failure to attack in force significantly diminished Lee's attacking force on the thirtieth and allowed Slocum to send reinforcements to his brothers fighting near the crossroads. Porter Alexander commented, "It seems incredible that this division [Huger's], within four miles of Lee, could have been allowed to spend the whole day in a mere contest of axemen." For Lee's army, the cost of the lost opportunity was great.[55]

Huger was not alone in failing to show initiative. Yet another Confederate general would fail to add any luster to his reputation this day. Theophilus Holmes had won a brevet for bravery in Mexico and had risen to the rank of major in the old army before he resigned on April 22, 1861. He had commanded a brigade at Manassas, and in early 1862, he was stationed in North Carolina, keeping guard against Burnside's presence in the North Carolina Outer Banks. On Sunday the twenty-ninth, Holmes responded to orders from the War Department and brought three regiments of Colonel Junius Daniel's brigade (1,750 men), plus two batteries of light artillery and 130 cavalry, across the James River. That evening, General John G. Walker's 3,600 effectives joined him, and they brought two additional batteries. They spent the night north of the river at Cornelius Creek. The following morning, when he received Lee's orders, he moved his troops to the heights at New Market and established "a position of great natural strength, covering the junction of the Long Bridge and River Roads." This was at about 10:00 a.m. Soon President Davis arrived and offered his approval to Holmes's selected position. His force was in an excellent location to protect the Confederate southern flank. General Henry Wise came up with troops from Chaffin's Bluff, and Holmes now had a force of about 6,000 men and six batteries of artillery.[56]

During the morning of the thirtieth, Colonel Thomas Rosser's Fifth Virginia Cavalry sent some pickets down the river road. They noticed that the head of the Federal column was moving "hurriedly and confusedly" and was just beginning to cross Malvern Hill. This was brought to Rosser's attention around 1:00 that afternoon, and he immediately sent word to Holmes and to Longstreet. Frustrated, Rosser noted that "for some reason or other no attention was paid to this report." He sent word to Lee, who came in person to see and ordered Holmes to attack. Seemingly in no hurry, it took Holmes until 5:00 p.m. to get into position, and by that time, the Federals were in solid strength on Malvern.[57]

While he had established a solid defensive position by the river, his lack of haste had eliminated whatever possibility Holmes might have had to seriously interrupt the Federal retreat. According to Porter Alexander, if Holmes had moved with dispatch he might have been able to occupy Malvern Hill. That is debatable, and even if that had been possible, the chance that he would have been able to hold it against the growing Union strength is highly unlikely. Holmes had arrived around 10:00 a.m. Porter stated that he had selected the position as early as 7:00 a.m., and his men had begun arriving at 9:00 a.m. He soon had two divisions of the Fifth Corps plus thirty-six guns, most of them rifled, in supporting distance. George Sykes's men were on the hill, and Gouverneur Warren's troops were taking position in the valley to the south of Malvern, across the river road, preventing a Confederate flanking action. Of his position, Sykes later commented that "nothing could be more commanding than the line I held."[58]

At about 4:00 p.m., Major R.K. Meade of the engineers saw Federal movement and rode up to Holmes to say that the enemy was "retreating in considerable confusion" on the road that crossed Malvern Hill. Meade recommended that a battery of rifled guns could be placed to "greatly embarrass" the Federals' efforts to retreat. Holmes ordered three sections of rifled artillery, six guns, to be moved two miles down the road and to be placed in a position to do just that. His chief of artillery, Colonel James Deshler, was sent with them, along with the 30th Virginia regiment of infantry from Walker's brigade. Holmes went forward to reconnoiter and started the remainder of his division forward. Soon he ran into Lee, who had just returned from viewing the Federal position. Lee approved of Holmes's efforts and directed that the artillery and infantry fire on the enemy's retreating columns. Porter said that Holmes's artillery placed itself in position to fire upon his own on the hill, and Holmes's infantry appeared ready to attack Warren.[59]

As Holmes's men marched down the crowded river road to support the artillery, they raised a dust cloud that alerted the Union fleet. The gunboats began launching their "awe-inspiring shells" into the Confederate column. The *Galena* and the *Aroostook* fired shells from their nine- and eleven-inch Dahlgren guns and one-hundred-pound Parrott rifles. Added to this were the shells from the rifled guns on Malvern Hill. D.H. Hill later commented that the shells didn't do great damage, but "they had a wonderful effect upon the nervous system." Porter Alexander later said, "[N]o fire is so appalling to unseasoned troops as that of heavy artillery received in a thick wood where every shot cuts limbs and smashes trees around them." Holmes's men, gathered in the woods, were now exposed to just such a fire, and it converged on them from opposite quarters. Part of Graham's Petersburg battery panicked and lost two guns and two caissons, and great confusion ensued. Some of the irregular cavalry stampeded, and only the efforts of veteran officers kept the inexperienced infantry from the same fate. Holmes's effort was falling apart. While it would be difficult to find humor in the situation, Theophilus Holmes managed to provide it. The half-deaf Holmes had gone into a small house, and as the shells shrieked all around, he came out of the building and said, "I thought I heard firing."[60]

Aware of the Confederate advance, the Federals were taking advantage of the natural strength of Malvern Hill. They had several batteries, and

Colonel Deshler estimated that Unionists had between twenty-five and thirty guns on the hill, as well as his own guns nearly in a crossfire. When he opened fire, the Federals returned it, and within an hour "they had pretty well disabled my battery." Men were wounded, and servicing the guns became problematic. He reported that two limbers and two caissons were blown up. Deshler was forced to withdraw his guns.[61]

The Federal fire continued, and the terrain would not permit a like number of Confederate guns to be brought into position to counter the Union cannons. Porter's artillery fired down on Holmes's guns, and Warren's men added a murderous infantry fire. Holmes thought that there was not much more he could do, as "the strength of the enemy's position and their imposing numbers were such that an attack upon them with my small force unsupported would have been perfect madness." His troops would have had to "march over three-quarters of a mile up a steep hill destitute of cover." In the face of Federal artillery, it could have meant slaughter. Events on Malvern Hill on the next day would verify that concern. At about nine o'clock that evening, he sent his men back near to where they had started, on the ridge near New Market Heights. Holmes's losses for the "Battle of Turkey Bridge" were two killed and forty-nine wounded.[62]

Added to Holmes's lack of initiative was a potentially more serious problem. During the confusion, he had requested reinforcements, and Longstreet sent Colonel Robert Chilton with orders for Magruder to march from his rear to go to Holmes's aid. This effectively removed Magruder's thirteen thousand men from the critical action at the crossroads. While they might add enough weight for Holmes to attack Malvern, timing would not permit that to happen. Guided by Chilton, Magruder marched his command to the river. Arriving near sunset, Magruder rode off to find Holmes. Unable to locate him, Magruder ordered his men to advance, to which General Semmes replied that it was too dark and the woods were too dense; units would become disorganized or worse. A short time later, Magruder received orders to march his men back to the Glendale area to support Longstreet's assault. While nothing of consequence was happening by the river, Longstreet and A.P. Hill would desperately need Magruder's troops during the climax of the battle, when Lee's campaign hung in the balance. Instead, Magruder's command was exhausted and wasted by marching to and fro. When the battle at Frayser's Farm was at its most desperate and victory could go to the side that threw in the most reinforcements, Magruder's thirteen thousand were nowhere to be found.[63]

Chapter 6

The Affair at White Oak

On the morning of the thirtieth, after leaving Savage's Station, Jackson's command continued to follow the retreating Federals. At about noon, they reached the northern crest of White Oak Swamp, a nearly impassable morass of muck, trees and vines. After a rain, the stream would swell and the bottom would be even muddier, and there had been rain the previous night. A Confederate recalled, "The hills descended by long and gentle declivities on both sides." Along the sides of the waterway the meadows were "soft and miry from the recent rains." On the northern (Confederate) side, in the field to the right of the road, there was an extensive farm with open fields, and on the left there was a "dense forest of pines." On the Federal side, there were open fields on both sides of the road, with woods behind, but the "low margin of the stream opposite the Confederate right was covered by a belt of tall forest, in full leaf, which effectively screened the Federals from view." Jackson had arrived on the north bank, and Union general Franklin remembered that "without exciting suspicion of his presence on our part, the whole movement being hidden by the woods."[64]

Franklin's men had destroyed the bridge crossing the swamp, and on the south side, he had posted an artillery detachment and Caldwell's brigade (of Richardson's division) in the open, opposing any attempt to cross. To the rear, concealed by trees, was the remainder of Richardson's division. They were posted to the east of the road. To the west, and farther back in an open field, was Baldy Smith's division. Interestingly, Franklin did not leave

White Oak Swamp. *Courtesy of the Library of Congress.*

a cavalry screen north of the swamp to detect any Confederate approach, leaving him effectively blind to the Confederate advance.

Jackson ordered his chief of artillery, Colonel Stapleton Crutchfield, to find a location to place his artillery, hoping to mass his guns to have effect on the enemy across the swamp. Only twenty-six years old in 1862, Crutchfield would later lose a leg at Chancellorsville and in 1865 would be killed at Sailor's Creek. He found an open position on the high bank, to the right of the road. Crutchfield needed to cut a road through some woods to reach it, which his men proceeded to do with dispatch. A total of about twenty-three guns were massed and, at 1:45 p.m., began open firing on the Federals on the far bank. Crutchfield mentioned Carter's King William Artillery, Rhett's South Carolina Battery and the batteries of Hardaway (Alabama), Balthis (Staunton), Nelson (Hanover) and Reilly (North Carolina). According to Crutchfield, they "opened suddenly upon the enemy, who had no previous intimation of our position and intention." Confusion reigned in the Federal batteries. They attempted counter-battery fire, but it was ineffective. Under the intense Confederate fire horses, mules and some teamsters panicked. Franklin said that the stampeding mules ran into a regiment of Meagher's brigade, "disabling more men than were hurt in the brigade during the remainder of the day." General William T.H. Books, commanding the Second Brigade of Smith's Division, said that the Confederate artillery "commanded the camp of the brigade that it was impossible for the troops to remain in it a minute." The batteries of Hazzard and Mott took the brunt of the fire, and their guns were silenced. Federal infantry and artillery quickly pulled back to the cover of woods but left one of Mott's guns behind.[65]

William F. "Baldy" Smith. *Courtesy of the Library of Congress.*

Once the Union artillery established its new position, about one thousand yards from the Confederate guns, they began to return fire. Hazzard was heroic, carrying ammunition to exhausted cannoneers. A limber was hit; the limber's horses had become entangled, and the wounded drivers were unable to extricate themselves. Hazzard was even taking turns loading one of his guns and was hit by a piece of shrapnel that shattered his leg. Taken from the field, he never completely recovered and died a few months later. Romeyn Ayers and Thaddeus Mott's batteries, with their longer-range rifled Parrott cannons, enjoyed some advantage in distance over the Confederates. Crutchfield remembered that it was difficult to determine the exact number and position of the Federal guns, as they were concealed in the wood. Of course, the Confederate position was by now well known. Crutchfield said that the Federal fire "was rapid and generally accurate, though the nature

Union artillery at White Oak Swamp Bridge. *From* Frank Leslie's Illustrated History of the Civil War.

of the ground afforded us such shelter to protect us from much loss." Hazzard's battery exhausted its ammunition, so Rufus Pettit's guns were ordered up from the Glendale area in relief and fired some 1,600 rounds. The artillery duel lasted until dusk "without intermission." For all of the metal thrown about that day, losses were relatively slight. The Confederates lost no guns or carriages but hit a Union caisson and exploded it. The next day, a Federal ten-pound Parrott gun and three caissons would be captured from the field.[66]

Union general William "Baldy" Smith vividly remembered when the Confederate batteries opened fire: "[O]pening the little outhouse, where I was, I saw that a great number of pieces had been quietly placed on the opposite bank, and they were throwing an immense quantity of iron—in fact the air seemed literally full of it." Trying to get his horse, he sought out his "Negro groom. I found he had taken my best horse in the direction of safety, and I saw no more of him or horse for two days."[67]

William Franklin recounted a story of the farmer who lived in a house within the Union lines. He had a young wife and a child of about two years and came up to Franklin and asked if there would be a fight. Franklin, of course, responded that "there certainly would be," and he estimated that it would begin in about half an hour. The farmer said, "I will have time to take my wife and child to my brother, who lives about a mile down the swamp, and get back before it begins." Surprised by this response, Franklin asked, "But why come back at all?" To this the farmer replied, "Why, if I don't your men will take all my chickens and ducks." Smith's headquarters was near the house, so it was a natural target for the Confederates. The farmer indeed returned. Several shots hit the house, one of which took off the man's leg. He bled to death in a matter of minutes. Franklin sadly commented, "He had sacrificed himself for his poultry."[68]

At the Nelson House, about two miles away, the intensity of the cannonade alarmed Sedgwick, and he sent two brigades, Dana's and Gorman's (Sully's), to Franklin's aid. The two brigades rushed to the scene, marching at least part of the distance at the double-quick. This left Sedgwick with only one brigade in reserve, but the threat at White Oak appeared pressing. Hopefully they would not be needed in the Frayser's Farm area that day.[69]

Jackson wanted to know the effect of the barrage and the situation on the other side of the swamp. Did the guns do their job? Would his division be able to cross? He ordered Thomas Munford's 2nd Virginia Cavalry to attempt it, accompanied by D.H. Hill and Jackson himself. A former student of Jackson's at the Virginia Military Institute, Munford voiced his doubts that the swamp could be crossed, to which Jackson sternly replied, "Yes Colonel, but you haven't tried it! Try it, Colonel!" The party advanced, and Jackson's curiosity was swiftly answered. As Munford remembered, "In we plunged, and there we floundered, belly deep to the horses in mud and mire, and the interlocking debris of the bridge, which had been destroyed and thrown in the creek, so as to impede our crossing." Having moved back to the wood line, the enemy battery was accompanied by "long lines of infantry," and these were able to pour fire on the destroyed bridge and the open area around it. The Federals opened on the Confederate scouting party with grape and canister, forcing the group back. Hill later commented wryly that "fast riding in the wrong direction is not military, but it is sometimes healthy." Clearly Jackson's men would not be able to cross at the bridge. On a lighter note, the scouting group had managed to capture one drunken Irish bluecoat. When asked if they should keep the prisoner or let him go, Hill ordered that they release him "to be a comfort to his family." He remarked, "That Irishman must have had a charmed life." Fired on four times at only fifty paces, "the only recognition that I could see the man make was to raise his hand as if to brush off a fly." A Federal solider later wrote that the story was indeed true, that the man had belonged to Company C of the 7th Maine Volunteers, and had said, "If he had one more canteen of whisky he could have held the position all day."[70]

Searching for an alternate way to cross, Jackson sent Munford downstream to look for an undefended crossing. Munford found a cow path and believed that infantry could cross there and sent word to that effect back to his commander. He later recalled, "I had seen his infantry cross far worse places, and I expected that he would attempt it." Wade Hampton located another crossing about a quarter of a mile away. At that point, the water was shallow and the bottom was sandy, and it was not more than ten to fifteen feet across. He saw the Federals lying down, relaxing and not expecting enemy action in that area. Things looked promising to Hampton, and he rode back to Jackson and said that he could build a bridge suitable for infantry to cross. Jackson instructed him to proceed. After completing the construction, Hampton returned and found Jackson seated on a log with his eyes closed. When Hampton stated that the ridge was ready, Jackson did not respond but instead rose and walked off in silence. Hampton was stunned and returned to his troops.[71]

Yet another possible crossing point was discovered. Ambrose Wright, of Huger's command, had been ordered down the New Road in search of Kearny's men and reached White Oak during the afternoon. Riding up to Jackson and asking for orders, Wright was instructed to retrace his steps and search for a place to cross upstream (to the west). A guide led him to Brackett's Ford, but the bridge was destroyed and trees were felled to block the crossing. Slocum's Federals were positioned on the far bank. Wright did not think it looked promising. Continuing three miles farther upstream, he located a potential crossing point at Fisher's house. However, it soon became dark, and he apparently did not advise Jackson of his find, nor did Jackson send a messenger to him. Appearances at Brackett's may have been deceiving. Franklin said that Jackson "ought to have known of the existence of Brackett's Ford, only one mile above White Oak Bridge, and ought to have discovered the weakness of our defense at that point." The Federal general said that had Jackson attacked at both Brackett's and in the White Oak area, he would have "embarrassed us exceedingly." Softening his tone a bit in defense of Jackson, Franklin commented that Jackson must not have been clear on Lee's expectations and poorly informed of the Federal weakness at Brackett's.[72]

After Hampton left, Jackson sat down under a tree, fell asleep and did not wake until after dark. Sitting down for dinner with his staff, he once again

Ayres' artillery at White Oak by Alfred Waud. *Courtesy of the Library of Congress.*

fell asleep. After a while, he rose abruptly and said, "Now gentlemen, let us at once to bed, and rise at dawn, and see if tomorrow we cannot do something!" All the while, Longstreet and A.P. Hill were just a few miles away, struggling ferociously to gain control of the Glendale crossroads. While crossing the swamp directly in the face of the Union guns and infantry was prohibitive, crossing elsewhere and threatening the Federal flanks would certainly have caused Franklin concern. Not being overly threatened by Jackson, he felt secure enough to release some ten thousand troops to the rescue of Federal troops desperately holding on farther south near Glendale. The crucial effect of this will be seen later. It was possibly the most disappointing performance of Jackson's career, and it came at the worst possible time.[73]

What had happened to Jackson? Much like the previous night, the legendary commander who was famous for pushing his troops and launching crushing attacks on the enemy seemed uninterested and totally exhausted. Many explanations have been offered for his behavior. D.H. Hill, Jackson's brother-in-law, who was present at the time, thought that "the labor of the previous days, the sleeplessness, the wear of gigantic cares, and the drenching of the comfortless night" had worn him down. Hill also suggested another reason, which was "Jackson's pity for his own corps, worn out after long and exhausting marches, and reduced in numbers by its numerous sanguinary battles." Hill said that Jackson "thought the garrison of Richmond ought now to bear the brunt of the fighting." He added that they didn't know that Longstreet and Hill were attacking without support or "that the firing that we heard was theirs." He even inferred that "Jackson's genius never shone when under the command of another." This would certainly be disproved at Chancellorsville the following spring! In any case, one of his comments is haunting: "[H]ad all our troops been at Frayser's farm, there would have been no Malvern Hill."[74]

Dr. McGuire, who knew Jackson as well as anyone in the army, said that the general was well known to strictly follow commands, and the direction Jackson had received was "to stay on this road until further orders." McGuire added, "If General Lee had wanted Jackson he could have sent for him, but General Lee did not want him." Jackson had to obey instructions—"as a soldier he could do nothing else." Adding some plausibility to this argument were Jackson's actions on the twenty-sixth at Mechanicsville, where he waited for orders at Hundley's Corner while A.P. Hill was fighting a few miles away at Beaver Dam Creek.[75]

Exhaustion is a recurring theme. Kyd Douglas wrote, "No one who rode with him on the 29th and 30th can recall a moment when he rested." Apparently, he had slept little since leaving the valley to meet with Lee and plan the campaign. One author pointed out that Jackson had written to his wife and said that he was sick with a fever, and a previous night he had a wet bed and had been awakened by a torrential rainstorm. Porter Alexander was having none of it. He said the rest of the army was just as exhausted. It had fought on the Peninsula and at Seven Pines, Mechanicsville and Gaines's Mill. He tended to agree with Hill's comment that Jackson pitied his own men. Alexander's comments noted that exhaustion certainly was a plausible factor and likely played a role in Jackson's less than effective behavior.[76]

Thomas Munford, who had known Jackson since the days at VMI, compared his chief's condition to Napoleon at Ligny, where, owing to exhaustion, "precious time was lost." Of Jackson, Munford said that "his devoted friends all agree that his endurance gave out, and that he was not at his best. His ambition was too great to flag, but neither man nor beast can go beyond certain limits."[77]

Jackson offered other reasoning. He said that he heard the heavy cannonading of Longstreet and was "eager to press forward." However, "the marshy character of the soil, the destruction of the bridge over the marsh and creek, and the strong position of the enemy defending the passage prevented my advancing until the following morning." By the morning of July 1, the Federals had retired toward Malvern Hill. Whiting's division then rapidly repaired the bridge, and Jackson's troops crossed over in pursuit. Jennings Wise concurred with Jackson's statement, stating that Jackson had opened his artillery barrage in an effort to gain superiority over the defenders, which did not occur. In his opinion, "Jackson undoubtedly recognized many elements of danger for his command and sought in vain to overcome them." While there may be some substance to Jackson's statement, Wise's does not hold up. Munford and Hampton had offered alternatives, and Jackson, as evidenced in the Valley Campaign, was not one to spare his troops when duty called. As he had demonstrated in the Valley, and would prove again in the future, Jackson did not fail to be creative in finding ways to defeat the enemy.[78]

Of all these explanations, a few stand out as the most likely. Robert K. Krick, a widely respected historian and student of Jackson, argued that he was "exhausted beyond the ability to function adequately" and that he "apparently hit bottom on June 30." He said that Jackson was a man who required adequate sleep. Completely worn down, he "simply was not at home." Many have noted Jackson's lack of rest since the time he arrived in Richmond, but one can look back even further. He had just fought the legendary but bone-wearying campaigning in the Shenandoah Valley. Getting little rest, he would fall asleep with his boots and sword on. Sandie Pendleton commented as far back as the first week of June that "General Jackson was completely broken down." One of Jackson's artillery battalion commanders, Colonel Thomas Carter, wrote that Jackson was "physically broken down, stupefied and dozed with fatigue." As exhausted as he had been in the Valley, there would be no opportunity for Jackson to rest before the action at White Oak.[79]

Krick also debunked D.H. Hill's notions that Jackson thought the Richmond troops should shoulder more of the brunt of fighting or that he was trying to protect his own troops. As Krick stated, "Jackson never before or after was unmanned by responsibility, prone to sulking, confused, jealous or unduly (if at all) sparing of his men. Quite the reverse was true in each case."[80]

Frank E. Vandiver echoed the theme of exhaustion, stating that "worked beyond the limit of even his iron endurance, Jackson did not realize that he had lost contact with reality." Vandiver also noted that Jackson had received orders from Lee that "pinned him to the road leading across White Oak Swamp, and he did not feel he should ignore Lee's desires." With no further word from his commander, Jackson may have assumed he was where Lee wanted him to be."[81]

Vandiver's explanation leads logically to an indictment of the command structure of the Army of Northern Virginia. Historians have noted how the entire Confederate Seven Days Campaign was a victim of poor communications. White Oak is a prime example. Why didn't Lee, who was probably within a forty-five-minute ride from Jackson, send a message to him and ask about his dispositions and request an attack? Why didn't Jackson write to Lee and request further instructions? What was discussed at their meeting? The answers to these questions were forever lost when these men passed away. In any case, it was a tragedy for the Confederate cause. The failure of Huger, Holmes and

Jackson to accomplish anything at all was a bitter blow to Lee's hopes to crush McClellan's retreating army. One could argue that because of the failures on June 30, a high price would be paid by Confederate troops the next day at Malvern Hill.[82]

Chapter 7

Time Is Running Out

By early afternoon, Lee's plan was rapidly deteriorating. Jackson remained immobile north of the White Oak Swamp with 25,000 men. Huger was doing nothing of consequence with his division, and Holmes was basically sitting tight on the southern flank. To make matters worse, Magruder's command, which had been designated to support Longstreet and A.P. Hill, was sent to Holmes's aid down by the river. Instead of having a pincers of 70,000 men converging on the Union army, Lee's attack would be limited to Longstreet and A.P. Hill, who had a combined force of about 19,200. This was not enough for the task at hand, and they would ultimately be outnumbered by Union troops. It was hardly a recipe for success.

The Federals had established a sort of "fishhook" line of defense. To the north, Franklin faced Jackson along White Oak Swamp. One of his Sixth Corps divisions, under William F. Smith, was stationed to the right of the bridge road, with Israel Richardson's division of the Second Corps to the left of that road. Henry Naglee's brigade from the Fourth Corps was with them. Moving to the west, Franklin's other division, commanded by Henry Slocum, was to the right of Charles City Road facing Huger. Across that road, to Slocum's left, was Phil Kearny's division of the Third Corps.

On Kearny's left, to the south, was George McCall's battered division from the Fifth Corps. McCall's men had been heavily bloodied in the actions on the twenty-sixth at Beaver Dam Creek (Mechanicsville) and on the twenty-seventh at Gaines's Mill; they were exhausted. By normal military protocol, they should have been stationed in a rest area. Instead, they were placed

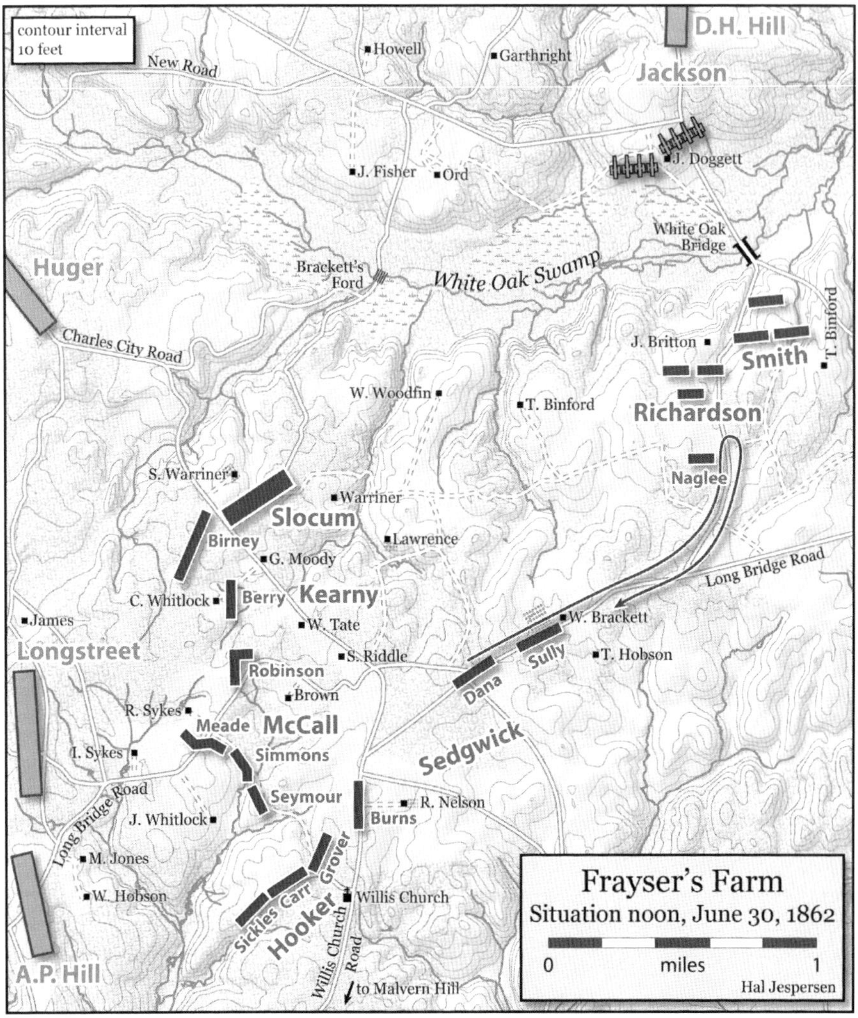

"Frayser's Farm." *Map by Hal Jespersen.*

astride Long Bridge Road, which would become the axis for the day's action. On McCall's left, farther to the south, was Joe Hooker's division from the Third Corps. Hooker's right rested on a farm road that entered the Willis Church Road a little north of the church. Behind McCall, across the Willis Church Road, John Sedgwick's division from the Second Corps, stationed in an open field in front of the Nelson House, could serve as a reserve. Fifth Corps commander Fitz John Porter had his remaining two divisions (Morell's and Sykes's) stationed farther south on Malvern Hill, where they had blunted

George McCall. *Courtesy of the Library of Congress.*

Holmes's efforts. The remaining divisions of Erasmus Keyes's Fourth Corps were safely tucked away south of Malvern Hill.[83]

It was a powerful position from which to guard the retreat of the trains, but it was complicated by its disorganization. All unit cohesiveness had broken down. As shown earlier, units were not with their assigned corps but instead were plugged in wherever they might be of use. The units were not organized into a contiguous defense; there were gaps between them. McClellan, the army's commander, once again was not on the scene. Instead, he had gone to the river to meet with the navy. Who was in charge? Corps and even division commanders would have to fend for themselves. It was a risky situation at the army's moment of greatest peril.

The storm that would soon break around the crossroads would be known by a variety of names. In the South, the spot would be remembered as Frayser's (sometimes Frazier's) Farm. Other names for it included Charles City Crossroads, Charles City Road, Glendale, Long Bridge Road, Nelson's Farm, New Market Road, Riddell's Shop, Turkey Creek, White Oak and Willis Church. The confusing names were appropriate, as the action soon to occur would be just as bewildering.[84]

Just southeast of the intersection of Charles City, Long Bridge and Willis Church Roads sat the Nelson farmhouse. While the Nelson family had long since acquired the property, to the locals it was still known by the name of the previous owners as "Frayser's Farm." At the time of the battle, two Nelson sisters lived there: Lucy, age sixty-two, and Ethelinde, age fifty-seven. Down and across the road a short distance sat the Willis Church. The Willis Church Road ran directly south to Malvern Hill. Several humble farms and homes were in the area, including the Brackett, Sykes, Atkins, Pleasants and Whitlock homes and Riddle's blacksmith shop. It was farm country with open spaces but included many wooded areas, thick undergrowth and some marshy places. It was an interesting and challenging place for a battle.[85]

During the movement south from White Oak, McCall had been ordered by McClellan to position his division so as to protect the army's supply trains as they moved down the Willis Church Road toward Malvern Hill and the river. It wasn't long before McCall realized that an attack on his position at Long Bridge Road would come from the west, from the direction of Richmond. Two of his brigade commanders, Generals Meade and Seymour, rode to the front and discovered that only a squadron of cavalry covered it. Receiving word of this, McCall ordered two regiments out to perform picket duty, the 1st and 3rd Pennsylvania Reserves. After studying the ground, McCall set his troops as follows: Meade's brigade was on the right, with his men astride and to the right of the road. To their front was Alanson Randol's Battery E of the 1st U.S. Artillery, with four twelve-pound Napoleon smoothbores, loaned from the army's reserve. Another section (two guns) of Randol's battery was held in reserve owing to a lack of space in the clearing but would soon be brought up. James Thompson's Battery G of the 2nd U.S. artillery, Kearny's division, guarded their right flank. While busy clearing brush to enhance his field of fire, Thompson was ordered to turn his guns to the right in order to support Kearny's troops. Randol then brought up his two remaining guns to

George Meade. *Courtesy of the Library of Congress.*

fill the space created. The 4th Pennsylvania Reserve infantry regiment was behind the guns in support, and backing the 4th were the 7th and 11th Pennsylvania Reserves.[86]

To the left of the Long Bridge Road was Truman Seymour's brigade. From right to left, Seymour posted the four guns of Kerns's Battery G of the 1st Pennsylvania Light Artillery, commanded by Lieutenant Frank Amsden. To his left was Cooper's Battery B of the 1st Pennsylvania with six guns. Next were two four-gun batteries of twenty-pound Parrott rifled guns, known as the "German" or "Dutch" batteries, from the army's reserve. Captains Otto Diederichs and John Knieriem led these. On a day that was filled with divided units, two of Knieriem's guns were in front of Diederichs's, and two were to the rear. Infantry was behind the guns in support, consisting of the 9th, 10th and 12th Pennsylvania Reserves. The 9th was behind Cooper, with the 10th to its left. The 12th would soon be posted on a ridge near a small log farmhouse known as Whitlock's. They hastily constructed a sort of defensive barricade out of some rails and logs found on the property. McCall commented that the ground in front of his division was a clear area, a "beautiful battleground" about eight hundred yards wide and one thousand deep, but it was too large for his force to adequately cover or be protected on its flanks. In reserve, McCall positioned Reynolds's brigade (1st, 2nd, 5th, 8th and 13th), which had been under the command of Colonel Seneca Simmons since the capture of Reynolds after Gaines's Mill. On his front line, McCall had about 5,000 men of his 7,500-men division, supported by twenty-four guns.[87]

"Fighting Joe" Hooker's division stood on McCall's left, near Willis Church. He, too, had received orders to protect the movement of the trains on the

Willis Church Road. Hooker's nickname actually derived from a misprint in a New York newspaper. The article read, "Fighting—Joe Hooker," but the dash was left out in print. Despite this, the name was appropriate. Very ambitious, the future army commander was hard-living and hard-fighting and was a top Federal division leader. Around 9:00 a.m., he established his line in an area behind the church, with Cuvier Grover and the First Brigade on the right, Joseph Carr's Brigade in the center and Dan Sickles's Brigade to the left. Grover placed the 16th Massachusetts on the right and to its left the 26th Pennsylvania. Behind them were the 1st Massachusetts and 2nd New Hampshire. The 11th Massachusetts was placed on the far left end of the division to protect against any effort by the Confederates to turn the division's flank. Carr's position included the 5th, 6th, 7th and 8th New Jersey. The 2nd New York was sent to the left of the division.[88]

Hooker gave directions for his artillery to "continue their march to our proposed camp on the James River, in order that they might be put in position there." At approximately 11:00 a.m., he noticed some wagons in his front, which were determined to belong to McCall's division. McCall's presence was a surprise to Hooker, and this was the first indication he had of it. Alarmingly, he noticed that there was a gap of five hundred to six hundred yards between McCall's line and his own; not only was there a gap, but the two divisions were also not properly aligned. Hooker noted that McCall's was in the woods at an "obtuse angle with the direction of my own."[89]

On McCall's right, Phil Kearny occupied a strong position in the space between Long Bridge and Charles City Roads. Thompson's battery was on the left, supported by John Robinson's Brigade. Robinson split the distance to Charles City Road with David Birney's brigade, which was on Robinson's right. In reserve was the brigade of Hiram Berry.[90]

James Longstreet was in overall command of the Confederate movement up Long Bridge Road, consisting of his division and that of A.P. Hill. Richard Anderson was assigned direct supervision of Longstreet's six-brigade division. While they marched, one of Longstreet's aides instructed A.P. Hill to take charge until Longstreet arrived. As his men approached the crossroads, Hill halted, established field hospitals and closed up his ranks. Anderson's men were about three-quarters of a mile in advance of his. Hill and Anderson rode the line and "made such dispositions as were necessary." Longstreet soon rode up and assumed command.[91]

As his men approached the crossroad, they encountered McCall's pickets. Longstreet ordered Colonel Micah Jenkins to clear them out, and Jenkins soon reported that the enemy was ahead in strength. Longstreet patiently

James Longstreet. *Courtesy of the Library of Congress.*

waited for the signal to advance, which was to come from Huger's expected attack on the left. "Everything was quiet on my part of the line, except for occasional firing between my pickets and McCall's." Around 2:00 p.m., "artillery firing was heard on my left, evidently at the point near White Oak Swamp where Huger was to attack." Assuming that this was the signal he was waiting for, Longstreet ordered "some of my batteries to reply, as a signal that I was ready to cooperate." The fire he heard was not the signal that Huger was launching an attack; it was merely his sparring with Slocum's guns. The coordinated attack was not happening. The Federals quickly returned fire. At that moment, Longstreet and Hill were speaking with Lee and President Davis, the latter having come out from Richmond to join them. They were sitting on their horses in an open field, surrounded by "tall, heavy timber and thick undergrowth," but an enemy battery had found their range. Several shells exploded near them, killing a few horses and injuring some more, and with strong encouragement from A.P. Hill, the "little party speedily retired to safer quarters." How amazed would the Federal gunners have been had they known that both the Confederate president and the army's commanding general were in their sights![92]

Lee soon rode off on his fruitless effort to have Holmes contribute, and Longstreet established his battle line. He ordered L. O'Bryan Branch's brigade from A.P. Hill's division to head for the right flank. To Branch's left would be James Kemper's brigade, with Micah Jenkins (commanding Anderson's brigade while Anderson led the division) on his left. Jenkins's line brushed the southern edge of the Long Bridge Road. Crossing that road, and to its north, was Cadmus Wilcox's brigade. Roger Pryor's troops were to the left rear of Wilcox, and Winfield Featherston's small brigade was to Pryor's left. Pickett's brigade, under the command of Eppa Hunton, was behind Jenkins and Kemper. With the exception of Branch's brigade, A.P. Hill's division was held back in reserve.[93]

Coming under continual fire from Federal artillery, around 3:00 p.m. Longstreet ordered Micah Jenkins to quiet the annoying enemy guns. While Longstreet thought it was understood that Jenkins would silence the cannons with sharpshooters, Jenkins, "second to none in either courage or ambition," was only too anxious for a dash at a battery. He went after the Federal guns with more intensity than Longstreet had intended, driving the Federal pickets of the 1st and 3rd, but was driven back by the 7th and 12th Pennsylvania Reserves. McCall then moved the 12th to the narrow timber on the left front of his line. General Truman Seymour ordered six companies of the 12th to occupy two log huts on the Whitlock property, and the others built up a rough breastwork made of log rails.[94]

Chapter 8

Desperate Fighting at Whitlock's Farm[95]

Lee soon returned from his meeting with Holmes. With little promise of help from the troops on the river road and still no hint of attacks by Huger and Jackson, time was running out. Porter Alexander noted that "for hours we stood there waiting—waiting for something which never happened. Every minute that we waited was priceless time thrown away." He lamented, "Our great opportunity was practically over, and we had not yet pulled a trigger." Lee only had one-third of his army on hand, but if he was going to strike a blow to McClellan's army, it was now or never. He ordered the attack.[96]

Longstreet commanded the attack to begin. James Kemper's brigade moved out first. Due to the lack of cohesion in the Federal command, there was not a contiguous line between McCall's left and Hooker's division. As luck would have it, Kemper would be heading directly for this weak point in the Union line. Were he able to drive through to the Willis Church Road, he could cut off the northern portion of the Federal army. Kemper sent his staff along the line to ensure that the advance was made in good order. He placed the 24th Virginia on his left, with the 7th, 1st, 11th and 17th in order, left to right. He put Arthur Rogers's Loudoun Artillery on a small elevation. The ground was uneven, "almost precipitous," a mix of open fields and thick woods, with undergrowth that entangled the men. The ground rose and fell, and it was swampy in places. Keeping lines in order was very challenging. For example, seven companies of the 17th were delayed for some time by the "nearly impassable nature of the swamp at the point at which they crossed."

Federal batteries were directly to Kemper's front, firing round shot and exploding shells at the attackers. As they pushed back the Federal pickets, Kemper's men were driven by the intensity of the enemy fire, and the whole brigade charged forward at double-time. Despite orders to the contrary, his soldiers sought to "reach the enemy's line by the directest route and in the shortest time." He added that "a more impetuous and desperate charge was never made than that of my small command against the sheltered and greatly superior forces of the enemy." Kemper's men crossed a swamp and then double-timed through the dense woods, despite his orders to the contrary. He realized that any effort to slow and re-form would be futile and would cause further confusion.[97]

After advancing between 1,000 and 1,200 yards, and going through yet more woods, Kemper's men came upon another clearing and the twenty-pound Parrott guns of the German (or "Dutch") Batteries. Two of John Knieriem's cannons were in front, with Otto Diederich's four guns about 100 yards behind them, to the left of the Whitlock house. Two more of Knieriem's guns were to the rear. In front of Kemper's brigade waited the six companies of the 12th Pennsylvania Reserves, posted in an "imperfect and hastily constructed breastwork and a house near by." Members of the 4th Pennsylvania Cavalry, fighting on foot, backed the 12th. Kemper remembered the attack, saying that the batteries and infantry "poured an incessant fire of shell, grape, canister and lead upon my line," causing serious damage. Captain James Cooper's battery, to the right, added to the fire. The men of the 12th, behind the log breastworks, fired volleys into the attackers.[98]

Kemper noted that "the left of my line was entirely unsupported, and greatly to my surprise and disappointment, for I had supposed that the movement of my brigade was part of a general advance along our entire lines." The lack of support was, in part, because his men had advanced too quickly; other troops were not yet in position. This problem would vex the Confederates all through the battle. None of the attacks would be properly timed, and units attacked singly instead of en masse. Poor coordination of attacks, owing in large part to the difficult nature of the ground, made proper communication and organization exceedingly difficult.[99]

David Johnston, of Company D, 7th Virginia, remembered, "[W]hen our brigade had cleared the woods, it entered, in a most confused state, an open field, at the farther side of which, some four hundred yards in front of us, was a Federal battery with heavy infantry supports." The shots from the enemy cannons "had been ploughing and ploughing through the woods from which we advanced to attack." Outrunning any support they might have had, the men were "rushing wildly upon the enemy, who quietly and coolly awaited our coming." He said that the Federals had laid out a trap for them, with guns in the front and infantry supports on the right and left.

Johnston continued, "If a reader has never been in a fierce battle he does not know how a man's courage is most severely put to the test." The men of his regiment were advancing from woods, over an open field, with no hope of shelter. Men would think "the enemy is posted in that lumber across the field, and before we move many yards he will open on us with shot and shell; this is perhaps my last day." Many were right. It would get worse; they approached the Federal position, and the shell was changed to canister. "Gap after gap yawns through the line, only to be speedily closed again." When they got close, they would be met with an avalanche of small arms fire. "As we go on men grip their muskets tighter; their eyes flash, their teeth shut hard, only to open with a cry of rage as they rush upon the guns and bayonet the cannoneers." J.P. Jordan remembered, "[A] rifle shot took away my haversack and canteen and severely bruised my left hip." Soon afterward, a ball broke his collarbone, and later he "was hit on the foot by another ball."[100]

Kemper's men drove on, firing into the defenders as they charged. Edgar Warfield, of the 17th Virginia, cited Porter Alexander's comments that it was difficult to control the line in the thick underbrush, but "the impetuosity of the charge broke the enemy's line." The Federals pulled back. With the Confederates firing at his battery from a distance of only sixty yards, twenty-two of Knieriem's horses had been shot, and he was forced to pull out his two forward Parrotts, the limbers and two of the caissons. He left his rear-most guns in place. Diederichs continued to blast away with canister and shells "used with very short fuse" until his ammunition was exhausted; then he, too, had to pull his four guns back. Colonel John Taggart, the commander of the 12th, said that the attackers tried to use a ravine to swing around his position. Fearing that they were about to be surrounded, the 12th hastily withdrew. Colonel James Childs of the 4th Pennsylvania Cavalry said that the 12th "broke in a most disorderly manner, without firing a shot at the enemy, and falling back upon the ranks of my men frightened the horses and compelled them to join in their disgraceful flight." He rallied his men a few hundred yards to the rear. Even though their line had been broken, the Federal fire had taken its toll. Kemper later wrote, "The ground which they gained from the enemy is marked by the graves of some of my veterans, who were buried where they fell…[showing] the points at which they dashed against the strongholds of the retreating foe."[101]

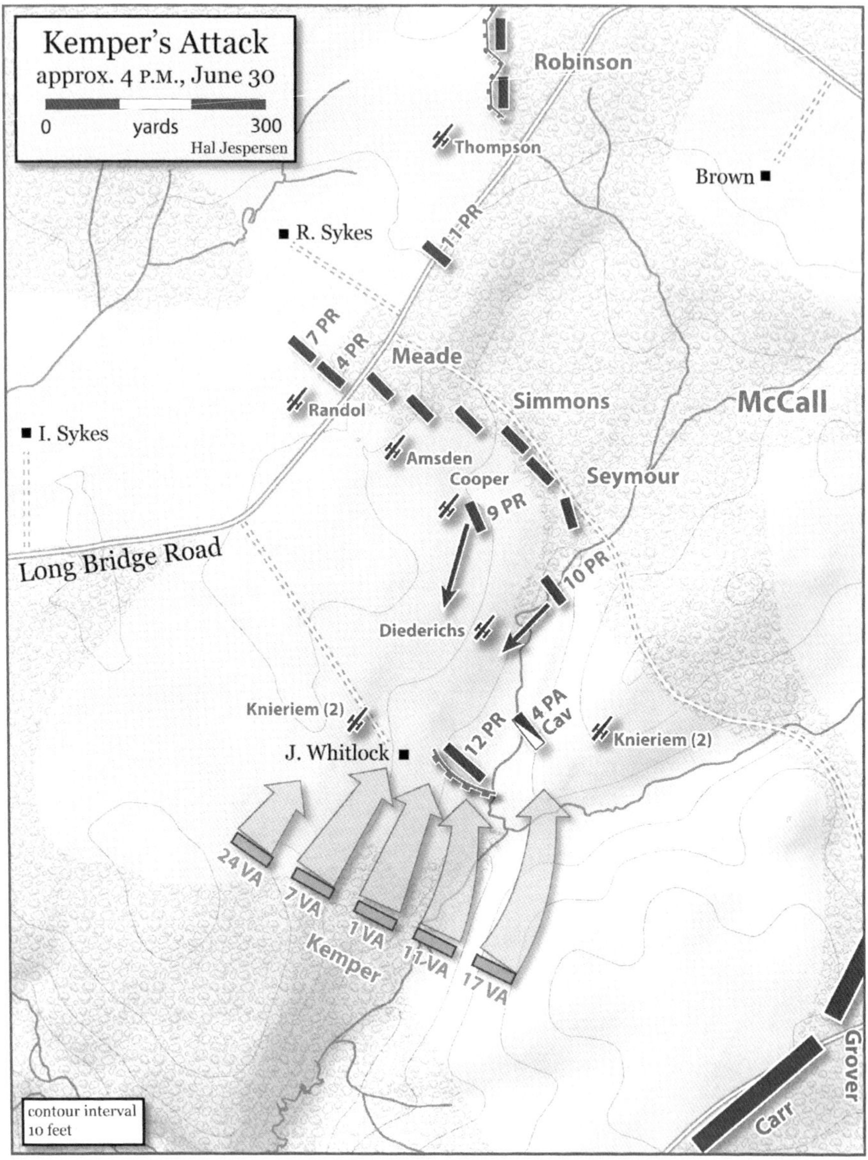

"Kemper's Attack." *Map by Hal Jespersen.*

The attack rolled on. Having broken McCall's line, Kemper's Brigade next approached the farm lane that led to Willis Church Road. Placed near the farm road was the First Brigade of Hooker's division, under the command of Brigadier General Cuvier Grover. His 16th Massachusetts Volunteers were to the immediate east of the road and "received and repulsed the heaviest and most persistent attempts of the enemy to break the lines." Grover noted that the "steadiness and determination" of his first line checked Kemper's advance and caused the attackers to withdraw.[102]

His men had captured McCall's line at the Whitlock farm, but Kemper could not hold without adequate support. Woods and underbrush encircled them, and Kemper was justifiably concerned about his precarious position. The Virginian said that "the inferior numbers which had alarmed the enemy and driven him from his breastworks and batteries soon became apparent to him, and he at once proceeded to make use of his advantage." With no reinforcements in sight, and with large bodies of the enemy on both of his flanks, Kemper had no choice but to pull back. His men began to retire in order, but soon things became more chaotic, requiring serious effort on the part of their leaders to maintain organization. Kemper sent out messages as to where to re-form, but the terrain made the task very difficult indeed and he would presently be hit by a Union counterattack.[103]

Not realizing that Kemper was about to pull back, McCall ordered Colonel Seneca Simmons to support the left. McCall also had called on his division's last reserves. Sumner's Second Corps had been stationed as a reserve near the Nelson house, but when two brigades, Dana's and Gorman's, had been sent to the White Oak Bridge area to support Smith against a possible attack by Jackson, it left only Burns's brigade of the Second Corps to back up McCall.[104]

Simmons had taken the 5th, 8th and 10th Pennsylvania Reserves and elements of other units from his right. At that moment, Jenkins was preparing to attack, and most of McCall's support facing Jenkins had been taken away. He would be in a precarious position if Jenkins were to advance. Moving to the left against Kemper's assault, Simmons formed his units for attack and said, "Brigade! Forward, Charge!" With bayonets fixed, the men "sprang up and with a savage yell, rushed madly." Colonel James Kirk of the 10th said that the horses of the retreating batteries caused "wild confusion" among his men. He plunged into the flank of the attacking Confederates, "completely routing the enemy, killing large numbers, and capturing about 60 prisoners." As for Simmons, his men begged him to get down from his horse because he was too easy a target. Unwilling to dismount, he quickly fell, mortally wounded. McCall's adjutant, Captain Henry Biddle, was also mortally wounded, hit three times as he tried to deliver orders. The Federals drove to the Whitlock house, and the Confederates attempted to re-form. Kemper and his officers did all they could do to organize their brigade, but they were forced to pull back. As he retreated, Kemper saw Lawrence O'Bryan Branch's brigade of A.P. Hill's division moving up on his right.[105]

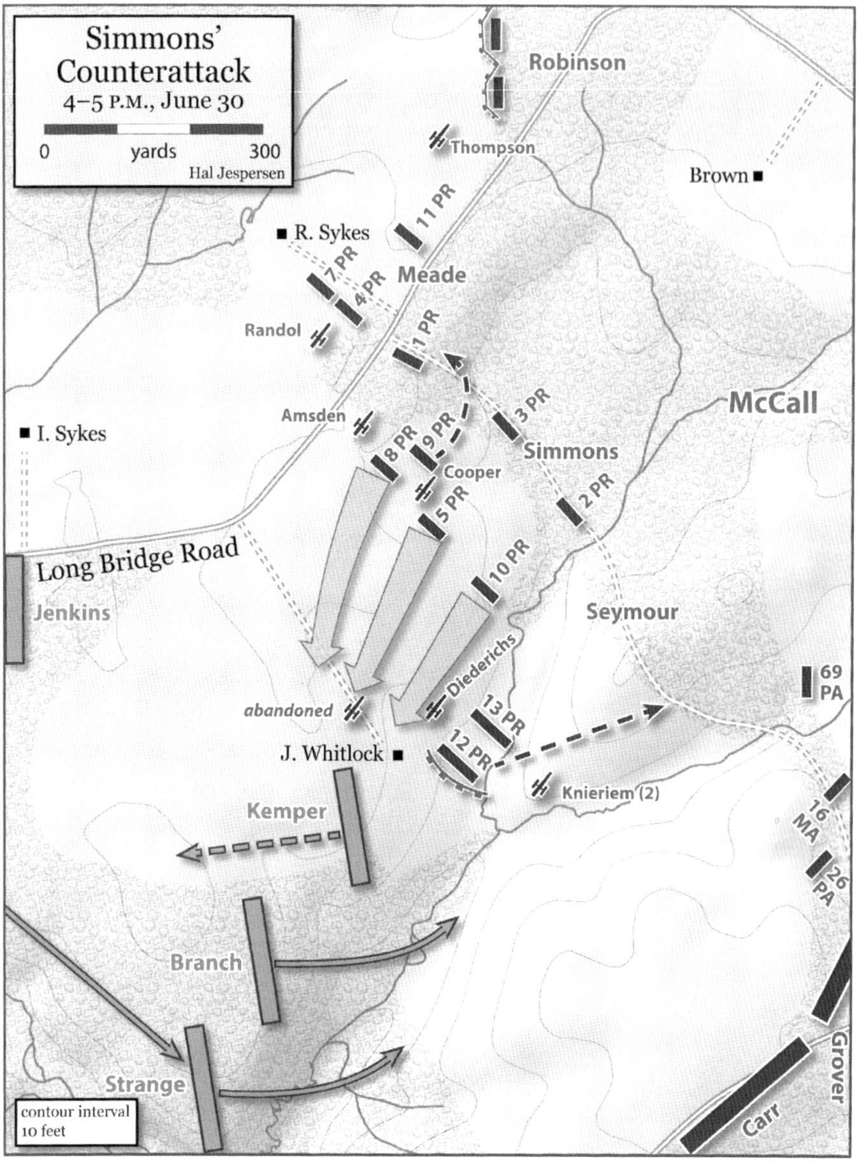

"Simmons' Counterattack." *Map by Hal Jespersen.*

Branch had been ordered to attack at the same time as Kemper, but his men were not ready. Further, he had to march through the confusing terrain, and consequently, he attacked late. He had no guide, but he "took the direction to whence came the shells." When they finally arrived on the field, Branch's men attacked and pushed the enemy back from the Whitlock house "for nearly a mile." While Branch's men certainly drove the defenders, a mile was an exaggeration—this would have pushed the Federals past east of the Nelson house by a few hundred yards. As his men were attacking the Federals, Branch noticed that the enemy troops were "rapidly accumulating as they fell back." He was advancing toward Hooker's line and saw the Union troops that extended past his flank. Branch was approaching the 26th Pennsylvania and the 2nd New Hampshire. George Wells, lieutenant colonel of the 26th Pennsylvania, saw that McCall "seemed to be holding his own, when suddenly he gave way and the attack fell upon our own lines." Owing to the nature of the ground, Wells could only bring the fire of one

Lawrence O'Bryan Branch. *Courtesy of the Library of Congress.*

company to bear upon the attackers, but in combination with the 2nd New Hampshire, it was enough to hold the attackers off. With the enemy in his front and on his flanks, Branch decided that it was best to rein in his attack and pull back. It was about this time that McCall ordered the companies of the 9th back to the support of Cooper to meet Jenkins's attack there.[106]

Pickett's Brigade was approaching the battlefield, marching up the Long Bridge Road. The commander, Colonel Eppa Hunton, had taken over General Pickett's brigade after the latter was wounded at Gaines's Mill but was quite ill himself. Command fell to Colonel John Strange. He moved the brigade to the right of the road and formed a line of battle. Captain James Dearing's artillery was to their front and firing, and the men were ordered to lie down. When ordered to advance around 5:00 p.m., they obeyed, advancing on Branch's right, but the terrain and the retreat of some of Branch's men made it difficult to keep the lines in order. The inability of Kemper's, Branch's and Hunton's brigades to coordinate was lamented by Kemper, who later said, "If it had been possible for these brigades to have advanced simultaneously with my own the victory of the day would have been achieved on the right of our line with comparatively little difficulty and at an early hour." The terrain had been consistently causing havoc on Longstreet's attack. Strange said that they had advanced "over such broken ground and through an almost impassable marsh, as well as encountering a brigade [Branch's] in full retreat, which forced its way through our ranks." Marching on, they were fired on by the enemy hidden in woods on their right. A shower of canister caused them to move by the left flank. The Confederates soon forced the four remaining companies of the 12th Pennsylvania Reserves to pull out, along with Diederich's four cannons.[107]

Strange's brigade emerged within a few hundred yards of the abandoned Federal guns and encountered a large force. At first, he assumed that they were friends, "until convinced to the contrary by the open, honest display of the old flag, whereupon I ordered a fire, and a charge drove them from the battery back to their line in the woods beyond." These were the guns in the rear section of Knieriem's battery. Strange was tempted to turn the recaptured guns on the retreating enemy but found that friendly troops were in his line of fire and decided to hold off.[108]

Strange continued to attack McCall's Pennsylvanians, driving them from the Whitlock area. Soon the brigade was within sight of the goal of seizing the Wills Church Road and cutting off the Federal retreat. As the last line of defense, Major Roy Stone of the 1st Pennsylvania Rifles saw the Federal troops in full retreat and ordered his men to lay down and allow the withdrawing troops to pass over them. His men then delivered a volley and continued to fire "for some minutes," but they were receiving murderous fire. Stone said his soldiers "were falling fast and I should soon have none left." He gave the order to retire "just in time to escape being surrounded." It was a desperate hour for the Union defenders in that sector, and at that time, their brigade commander, Truman Seymour, decided to wander off in the direction of Franklin at White Oak, possibly seeking assistance.[109]

Private Tobias Yoder of the 10th Pennsylvania's Company A was one of the lucky ones that day. A buckle had been shot from his hat, and a shell fragment had hit his coat. Quickly he was hit by seven bullets, two piercing his lungs, one of which shattered his shoulder blade. Two of the bullets passed through his blanket roll and hit him in his side. One lodged in his hipbone and another near his spine. Amazingly, he survived. Captured and sent to prison, he lived until the age of seventy.[110]

During a lull in the fighting, Private Warfield began to look after the wounded. Coming upon a Union soldier with a scalp wound, his "attention was attracted to the cap he had with him." Quickly recognizing the name cut into the visor as having belonged to his brother, Warfield asked where the Yankee had come into possession of it. The wounded soldier replied that "he had lost his own and had taken this one from a dead Confederate soldier lying near him." Warfield asked whether the soldier had really died, to which the Yankee replied, "They had both fallen within arm's reach of each other." The Yankee and Warfield's brother had started the attack about thirty yards from each other. Warfield discovered that his brother "fell, shot through the breast, and was bayoneted in the stomach after he fell." During the same lull, Federal soldier G.W. Wilson saw a Federal soldier have mercy on a wounded Confederate by taking him water. As soon as he left the spot, three Confederates fired on him. The soldier's comrades quickly captured those doing the firing. Regardless, the merciful soldier would be wounded himself shortly afterward.[111]

Seeing how close the Confederates were to seizing the Willis Church Road, Second Corps commander Edwin Sumner sent an urgent message to the White Oak area to recall Dana's and Sully's brigades, which would have to hurry two miles in the heat, over dust-choked roads, in order to arrive in time. Fortunately, Sedgwick had sent for them at the first sign of trouble, and they were already on their way, double-timing as often as possible. Sumner then sent in his final brigade, that of William Burns. Burns had four regiments, and he ordered the 69th and 106th Pennsylvania to Hooker's right, along the farm road that ran to the east of the Whitlock place. Edmund

Kirby's battery was set up on a rise near the Nelson house, with the 72nd Pennsylvania positioned to its right and the 71st placed behind. Despite some of McCall's men approaching him, retreating in confusion, Kirby opened fire with solid shot and shell. He stated that the attackers "did not approach nearer than 500 yards to my position, but kept up a terrible fire of artillery and musketry upon us from their position in the woods, where they lay concealed."[112]

Burns's reinforcements from White Oak soon began to arrive. Dana said they had double-quicked over the two-mile distance "to make all possible haste. Very many men broke down on the road, and those who arrived at Nelson's farm, although in excellent sprits, showed the marks of great fatigue." They had hurried over the road where "dust was so thick a man could not see ten feet." These were the same men who earlier in the day had rushed to the bridge to support Franklin. The 19th Massachusetts rested for just a moment and then drove into the wood line. The 20th Massachusetts, 7th Michigan and 42nd New York joined the force temporarily commanded by Colonel William R. Lee, who was leading for Dana. The four regiments advanced, but the ground was sloped and enemy fire played havoc with the unit order. They had to stop three times to redress lines. Corporal Isaac Sampson, a twenty-year-old farmer of Company K of the 20th Massachusetts, lost his leg to a round shot. Sergeant Compass had his breast and bowels torn away by an exploding shell. The 19th Massachusetts was separated from the others as it allowed a battery to pass. To the right of the now three-regiment attacking formation was the 20th Massachusetts, with the 7th Michigan on its left and the 42nd New York beside the 7th. Colonel Lee was soon knocked out of command, as he had a hard collision with an artillery horse and was not able to lead. Major Revere took over the lead (he would have two horses shot from under him).[113]

As they advanced, the attackers came upon the abandoned German batteries and saw the horses torn by the shells, some still alive in agony, kicking and screaming. The ground was strewn with dead and dying men. Soon the advancing Federals ran into concealed defenders, who unleashed a volley on them. The 7th Michigan returned a volley and then broke for the rear, joined by the 42nd New York. The 20th Massachusetts continued to exchange fire with Branch's men, and it was bloody work. Private Jared Hunter was hit by a shot that had already passed through the neck of the man in front of him. Hunter died silently and instantly. Soon the Confederates began to flank the 20th, and they were forced to withdraw. Twice they paused to fire a volley at their attackers and ultimately formed a line farther to the rear.[114]

Burns led the 72nd Pennsylvania in. Colonel Edward Hinks of the 19th Massachusetts took his exhausted regiment "into the dense woods…up a very steep hill, some 150 yards, against a murderous fire." One soldier remembered, "We then advanced in line of battle at the double quick toward the woods, the bullets flying thick and fast, piercing clothing" and worse. They ascended a hill with "the woods being so thick that it was not only impossible to keep our formation in line of battle, but also impossible to see more than two lengths of a Co. either way." Burns threw the 19th Massachusetts and the 71st Pennsylvania into the area recently vacated by the 7th Michigan and 42nd New York. They soon came upon the enemy on "the crest of the hill not ten yards distant." He ordered his men to fire and then "received the fire of the enemy breast to breast." The enemy were "not ten feet away…and poured a terrible fire into our ranks. In this one volley about 80 of our men were either killed or wounded." Soon men were seen coming out of the woods, and Colonel Hinks asked, "What men are these?" His answer was a shower of bullets. Hinks was wounded in the thigh and had to leave the field. Because of the illness of Lieutenant Colonel Devereux and the mortal wounding of Major How, the command of the regiment fell to Captain Edmund Rice. Rice remembered that the enemy "poured a volley upon us at so short a range that our men's faces were in many instances singed by the flash of the enemy's muskets and on the right of our regiment some of our men crossed bayonets with the enemy." Of Major How, Rice said that his wound was "the highest praise which can be spoken of a true

Bayonet check. *Courtesy of the Library of Congress.*

John Sedgwick. *Courtesy of the Library of Congress.*

patriot." The major said, "Let me die here on the field. Tis more glorious to die on the field of battle."[115]

The Federals saw a Confederate regiment "not ten feet from our left" and another one on the right, and "the rebels at once rose and poured a terrible volley into our ranks. In this one volley about 80 of our men were either killed or wounded." Quickly recovering, they returned fire but "could not stand it for long" and had to pull back. Dana took his old regiment, the 1st Minnesota, into the woods, followed by Sully's 15th Massachusetts. The 34th and the 82nd New York maintained their positions. Sedgwick was wounded in the arm and in the leg and had two horses shot out from under him.[116]

Hooker saw Seymour's men retreating, "completely routed, and many of the fugitives rushed down the road on which my right wing was resting." Some ran through his lines "and actually fired on and killed some of my men as they passed." Hooker had grave concern about the disastrous effect this could have on his lines and was relieved when they had passed through. Strange's Confederates were close behind but were stopped by the fire of the 16th Massachusetts Volunteers and the 69th Pennsylvania Volunteers, who hit the attackers' flank with rifle fire. "Whenever the enemy ventured to uncover himself from the forest, a destructive fire was poured into him along my right

Joseph Hooker. *Courtesy of the Library of Congress.*

wing." Cuvier Grover then took the 1st Massachusetts, and Joshua Owen led the 69th Pennsylvania into the open field on the Confederate flank, attacking with great and almost reckless daring. A member of that unit later remembered, "The Sixty-ninth poured volley after volley into them, keeping up a ceaseless and irresistible fire." Owen ordered his men to fix bayonets and said, "Up, Sixty-ninth, and at them!" The regiment instinctively rose with a cheer, jumped to their feet and charged up the hill at the double-quick. "Thc enemy didn't like the looks of that line of steel, and in his turn was forced to retreat, leaving his dead and wounded behind him." Sumner's brigade commander, William Burns, said that the 69th "pursued the victorious rebels back over the ground through which they were passing and crowned the crest of the hill where McCall had lost his artillery. Gallant Sixty-ninth!"[117]

The 2nd New Hampshire and the 26th Pennsylvania soon joined Grover. His men suffered severely from the enemy's fire, but they broke Strange's attack. Eventually, Grover's force would be withdrawn to its original position in Hooker's line. Hooker remembered, "The loss of the Rebels in this battle was very severe. The field on which it was fought was one of unusual extent for the numbers engaged, and was almost covered with their dead and dying."[118]

Chapter 9

The Struggle for the Center

While Kemper's attack on the right had moved out ahead of the rest of the division, fighting soon spread to the center and left. Micah Jenkins advanced toward Lieutenant Frank Amsden's 1st Pennsylvania Light Artillery Battery G and Captain James Cooper's 1st Pennsylvania Light Battery B, both positioned to the south of the Long Bridge Road. Their guns were ready to receive Jenkins warmly with canister.[119]

With the 4th and 5th South Carolina to his left and the Palmetto Sharpshooters and the 2nd South Carolina Rifles to his right, Jenkins approached Amsden and Cooper's position. The Federal batteries were about two hundred yards south of the road, with an open field of a few hundred yards to their front and a wood line to their rear. The 6th South Carolina had been deployed as skirmishers. McCall had moved the 9th Pennsylvania Reserves to the left to meet Kemper's attack, and Cooper and Amsden's batteries were only thinly supported. The 1st and 3rd Pennsylvania Reserve units quickly began to fall back. Cooper saw the Confederates advancing toward him, and his ten-pounder Parrott rifles opened on them, joined by Amsden's guns. Charging artillery in an open field, Jenkins's men were hit hard. Jenkins himself had his sword shot off, his overcoat was hit several times by shell fragments, he was wounded in the shoulder by a piece of shell and he had two horses shot out from under him. A veteran of the 1st Pennsylvania Reserves wrote, "The batteries thundered volley after volley." The Confederates rushed at them in a massive column from the wood and, with a fiendish yell, came swarming across the field. The artillery tore terrible gashes through the enemy's ranks, covering the ground with the dead.

Micah Jenkins. *Courtesy of the Library of Congress.*

The gunners loaded double, even triple charges of canister, the guns recoiling with so much force that they endangered the lives of those around them.[120]

Cooper's fire was joined from across the road by Randol's six Napoleon smoothbores. J.R. Sypher called the fire "the most terrific storm of grape and canister, that ever whirled in death-torrents across fields of fiercest battle." They charged in masses, approaching the guns "at point-blank range, with charges of double shotted grape and canister." The fire plowed "a horrible furrow of flesh and gore through the living field." Adding to carnage inflicted by the enemy guns, the terrain also was a serious challenge for Jenkins, as the trees and undergrowth made it difficult to keep his unit in formation. He came upon one of his men who was afraid to advance and who said it was "too hot in there…the bullets fly too thick." Jenkins upbraided him, saying, "Go back sir and don't disgrace yourself."[121]

Amsden's guns soon ran low on ammunition, and he sent for his caissons. Unfortunately for the Federals, Seymour had taken the precaution of ordering Amsden's caissons to the rear shortly before Jenkins's attack but had failed to tell the battery commander where they were being sent. Stunned that they could not be found, Amsden ordered a lieutenant and two buglers to search for them, but they could not locate the missing ammunition. He reported this to McCall, who ordered him to the rear. Their guns would soon be missed.[122]

While watching Jenkins's attack, Porter Alexander saw a "tall, handsome, young fellow" drop out of the ranks and approach him. "As he seemed weak I went to meet him & found he had been shot through the lungs, the bullet passing clear through." He had been his unit's color bearer. Alexander had a flask with some of his father's "Old Hurricane brandy of 1811" and gave him some and then helped the soldier to an ambulance. When the wounded man asked if he might survive, Alexander told him the story of a soldier who had been shot through the lungs at Bull Run and had lived. The wounded soldier replied, "I'm willing to die for my country if I must; but I'd a heap rather get well & see my mother & folks again." Alexander never saw the man again but always wondered if he had made it through.[123]

McCall shifted the 9th Pennsylvania back from his threatened left to retake the position. Colonel Jackson, commanding the 9th, said that his men "deeply sympathized with the captain [Cooper] in his loss, I at once determined to recapture the guns." He re-formed his regiment and advanced. As they did, they moved through the debris and "carcasses of horses and bodies of men, inextricably mixed." The captain of the 9th, John Cuthbertson, remembered the fight: "A hand-to-hand struggle ensued; muskets were clubbed and bayonets were used, the enemy was driven from the guns." A "supernatural frenzy fired the spirits of the men. The shouts of command, the shrieks and yells of the enemy…the thrust and parry of the bayonet, the crash of the clubbed musket, the spouting of blood, the death cry." It was an evening of horror. After he was wounded in the thigh and carried from the field, Cuthbertson said that the men fought "with a recklessness of life" that astonished him. The 9th pushed the Confederates back temporarily, but the fighting was not yet ready to end. The seesaw battle for the guns would continue[124]

Jenkins and his men continued on, attacking and being driven back by the volleys from Seymour's men. The Confederates relentlessly continued their assault. Joined by the 9th and 10th Alabama of Wilcox's Brigade, Jenkins's men finally began to drive the Federal defenders. As he rode over the works of Cooper's infantry supports, Jenkins's horse was shot from under him. The Confederates stormed up to the enemy defenses, and the struggle became hand-to-hand, involving bayonet thrusts and swinging muskets crushing brains. Soon the remaining Federals abandoned the position, retreating a few hundred yards and regrouping. Cooper's men tried to limber the guns so as to get them safely out, and Jenkins yelled to his men to "shoot down their horses!" so that the cannons could not be pulled from the field. With most of the horses down, the Federal gunners retreated, leaving their battery behind. Jenkins's men then turned the guns on their former owners. As the Confederates moved through the guns, they drove through infantry fire, as well as artillery on their flanks. Scores of men were falling to the fire from the infantry and the guns. One soldier remembered the terror: "The sullen 'thug' of the grape shot as they bury themselves into the bodies of the men is an appalling sound—one that can never be forgotten…whole companies are decimated."[125]

One Union soldier, James Maxwell Sloan, recalled his capture. He had taken a moment to try to help one of his fellow soldiers, who "asked me something in an unintelligible tone I could not understand. I bent over him and asked if I should give him some water." After providing the water, Sloan moved on, promising to send aid. Soon he happened upon a single Confederate soldier who "appeared somewhat startled, but stood still, never attempting to use the excellent rifle he carried." They had a conversation, and the Union solder ordered the Confederate to throw down his rifle. "He made no movement towards a surrender, but pointed me to where his friends were and hailed them. And sure enough I saw for the first time a whole regiment of Rebels just a few paces off." Realizing his dilemma, "an involuntary sentence burst from my heart, and all I could say was, my God, this is awful."[126]

Truman Seymour. *Courtesy of the Library of Congress.*

A correspondent for the *New York Tribune* described the scene:

> *The foe coming from the dense forests, rushed…with a recklessness and contempt for death that has surpassed the desperation of all other fields. In*

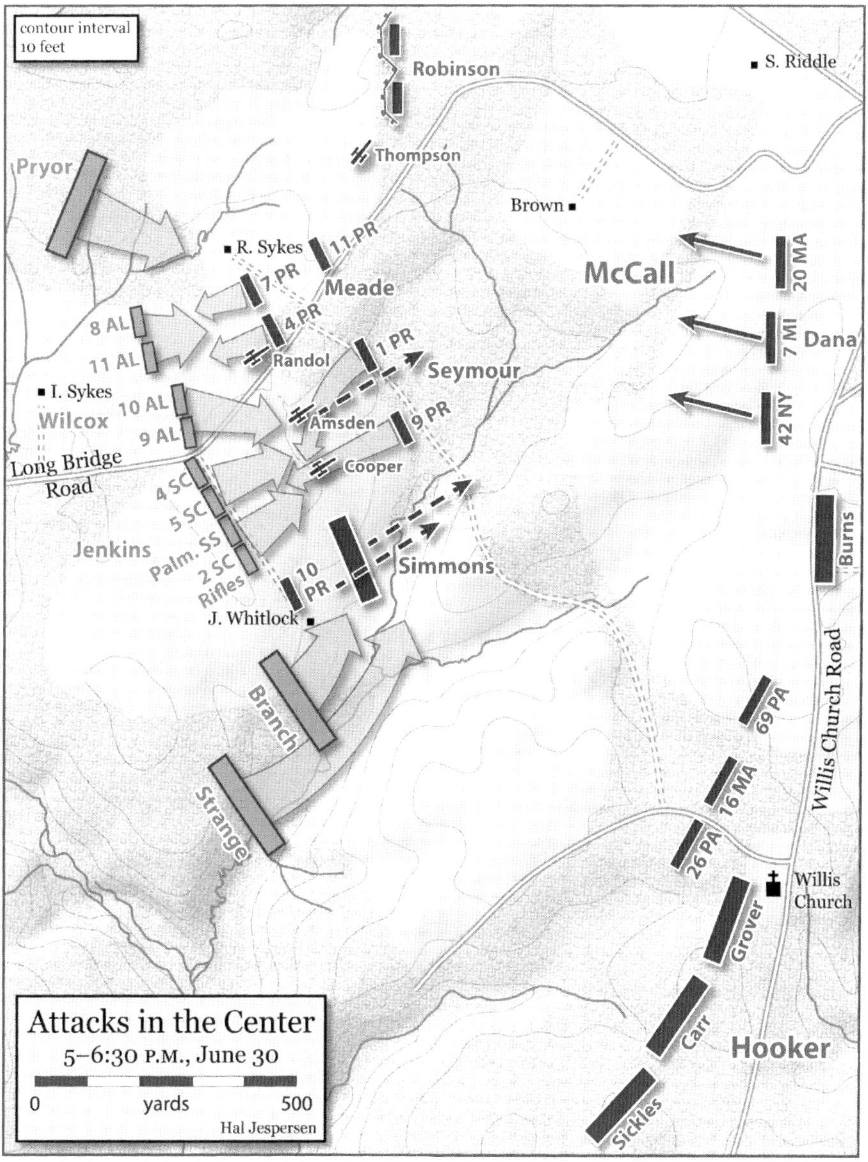

"Attacks in the Center." *Map by Hal Jespersen.*

Scene along Willis Church Road. *From* Frank Leslie's Illustrated History of the Civil War.

> *an hour like that, when men in dense masses, maddened with the excitement of battle, rush upon the fiery ordnance that at every round for a distance of a thousand yards, at point blank range, with charges of double shotted grape and canister, plows a horrible furrow of flesh and gore through the living field, artillerymen, like demons incarnate, revel amid blood, groans, destruction, death, mangled forms, and fumes of hell.*[127]

Richard Ervin of the 6th South Carolina remembered being wounded in the attack: "We swept on nearing the battery, just then I fell." He was shot near his left shoulder, "the ball going through all of my clothing and stopping on a rib near my heart." Ervin was holding the flag, and it was clutched firmly in his left hand. He "had lost all power" in his hand and could not loosen his grip. "When I was hit by the ball, it felt like a red hot iron was run in to me. I was knocked to my knees and could not see for a few seconds." Ervin's thoughts turned to home and to escaping the battlefield. "I hugged my broken arm close to my body, and turned to the left, where I would soon be down a hill and less exposed to shot and shell."[128]

In his report, Jenkins stated that he had advanced far enough to take "command" of the Willis Church Road: "I had a very strong position and with my weakened numbers could have made it good for some time." (Jenkins was within firing range of the road but had not physically reached it. Being close enough to fire on it effectively gave him command of the road.) The young Jenkins, only twenty-seven, was overcome by the slaughter. He had roughly 1,000 men in the spring, but since Seven Pines, his brigade was now reduced to only 125. Thomas J. Goree, one of Longstreet's staff officers, remembered that Jenkins was "weeping like a child" over the fate of his men. Goree said that Jenkins told him that he had prayed that he would share in their death.[129]

Chapter 10

Havoc at Randol's Guns

Cadmus Wilcox's brigade had arrived around 2:00 p.m. It was clear that Federal troops were in his front, and his brigade, along with Pryor's and Featherston's, was ordered to advance about one mile to the edge of the woods. He was to the left of Jenkins, across the Long Bridge Road. His brigade had a clear field in front of them. Wilcox threw skirmishers out, feeling for the enemy, and waited in position for three hours. Around 5:00 p.m., Federal artillery began firing; "shot and shell passed over and fell beyond us, some exploding near us." One of his batteries returned the fire, but owing to the wooded terrain, little damage was incurred by either side. Around 5:40 p.m., Wilcox saw Hunton's (Pickett's) brigade moving across the open meadow, and then he was ordered to form his brigade in the field, while Featherston was to his left, shifting to the left to reach Huger, who was expected to be attacking.[130]

Ordered by Anderson to press forward, Wilcox was instructed to shift to the left to keep in touch with Featherston. He was ordered forward and again was told to shift to the left. One more time he received both instructions. Following this confusion, he ultimately was ordered to press forward. Wilcox knew nothing of the strength of the enemy in his front and knew little of the terrain. Then the command came: "Forward…every man was on his feet, and with a savage yell sprang into the opening. With all possible speed" they rushed forward through the field, "guided alone by the artillery fire of the enemy," which passed over them, still causing little damage. Soon they entered more woods, which were so "thick with undergrowth that a forward

Cadmus Wilcox. *Courtesy of the Library of Congress.*

movement in line of battle was impractical." By constantly adjusting his angle of approach, Wilcox was able to reach a more open area. Wilcox said that the trees and undergrowth were so thick that he couldn't see his men on the left or on the right. Randol's guns were blasting away at them. Many of his men "had their lives snuffed out by iron missiles hurled from those blazing cannon." Still they pressed on. Two of his regiments, the 9th and 10th Alabama, had crossed over the Long Bridge Road where it curved and joined Jenkins in the attack on Cooper's battery. The 8th and 11th Alabama, plus four companies of the 6th South Carolina, stayed to the left of the road, which descended and crossed a small stream. The area was boggy, "with a dense growth of trees in it, rendering it difficult for the regiments on this side to make their way through it." The cannons of Alanson Randol's six-gun Battery E of the 1st U.S. Regulars had been facing toward the attack on Cooper, but now they were turned toward the Alabamians. Thompson joined in with his six guns. Behind Randol's guns, between them and their caissons, were the 4th, 7th and 11th Pennsylvania Reserves. The Confederates came on and at three hundred yards were met with the "frightful havoc" of Federal canister, with "the grape shot coming thick and fast through the trees."[131]

After making their way across the stream and through the brush, Confederates marched up a slight rise for some distance and reached more open ground. The enemy was posted in the woods to the left of the field and, according to Wilcox, "opened a brisk and close fire upon the regiment of my line." As the Confederates reached the open area, the first thing the Federals saw were the tips of their flags and then slowly, step by step, the flags themselves. The 4th Pennsylvania Reserves lay hidden in the tall grass, waiting until the enemy approached within sixty yards, and then the order was given "to rise and fire." Sergeant James Chester remembered, "We were ready for the onslaught…the guns were double charged with canister… Napoleon guns at canister-range are impregnable, if properly served." A deadly fire was poured into the attackers. The 8th Alabama halted and returned fire. Colonel Albert Magilton, commanding the 4th Pennsylvania Reserves, remembered that his fire forced the Confederates back, but it was quickly returned, driving the 4th rearward. The 8th Alabama continued moving toward the guns, but Randol kept up his deadly fire. Magilton rallied his men, and the seesaw struggle continued, as the combined power of the battery and infantry once again drove off the attackers. Again the Confederates re-formed and charged. Randol said that his guns, combined with firing from Thompson's six cannons, inflicted "great slaughter" on the attackers. Joined by the fire of the 4th, 7th and 11th Pennsylvania Reserves, the Federals held Randol's battery for the moment.[132]

To its right, the 11th Alabama reached the open area, which was a space of about three hundred yards to its front. About one hundred yards to the north of the road stood the home of Isaac Sykes, and about two hundred yards beyond that was Randol's battery, with a clear field of fire. The 11th Alabama advanced into the open field and was in plain view of Randol's guns. It received punishing fire: "This battery began at once a rapid discharge of grape and canister upon this regiment." The 11th advanced to within two hundred yards of the enemy cannons, "gave loud cheers, and then rushed for the guns." Randol's guns responded by tearing fearful gaps in the attackers. At one hundred yards, the Alabamians halted for a moment and aimed a "well directed fire" into the battery and the troops behind it. They then continued their rush

Alanson Randol. *Courtesy of the Library of Congress.*

toward Randol's position, but the defenders were pouring fierce fire into their front and their flank.[133]

Randol was firing canister into the Alabamians and remembered how they "came boldly on, notwithstanding the frightful havoc made among them." The fire from Randol's guns swept a channel of death through the mass of men, but they continued on. Federal fire threw them back. Randol's infantry supports rose to countercharge, and Randol cautioned them that if they "were obliged to fall back, they should at once unmask my fire by returning by the flanks of the battery." They indeed charged but were driven back by the Confederates, who continued their attack. The chaos and panic of battle caused them to forget their training and Randol's instructions. Albert Magilton of the 4th Pennsylvania Reserves said, "Finally my regiment broke and scattered in the woods." General McCall even made an attempt in vain to rally them. As they retreated, the Federal infantry supports ran directly at the battery instead of retreating by the flank, and Randol said, "I in vain endeavored to make them unmask my fire." He was unable to shoot his lethal canister at the onrushing Confederates, and suddenly the attackers were among his guns. Randol ordered the Napoleons to be taken to the rear, but the attackers had shot thirty-eight of his horses. Thompson's battery of Kearny's division was on Randol's right rear, in line with his limber chests, firing at the attackers. The combination of that fire and the number of horses wounded or killed made it impossible for Randol to get his guns out. He ordered the limbers to be driven to the rear and saved. By the time he collected his battery in the rear, Randol found that he had lost six guns, four caissons, two limbers and forty-six horses.[134]

Among the soldiers killed was Samuel W. Lascomb of the 7th Pennsylvania Reserves. Of his death another veteran wrote, "The death pallor began to gather on his face, but he fixed his glazing eyes upon the colors and said 'I die happy.'" Lascomb was among so many killed this day. The same veteran remarked, "His brave young heart ceased to beat, and he a corpse on the battlefield…there was no one so true to his country and its flag." Sadly, the same could be said for so many men that day.[135]

The 11th Alabama had suffered dearly in taking the guns and was not about to submit to enemy efforts to retake them. Federals were "under the cover of trees on our left flank and directly in our front, confident and bold in their superior strength." Randol rallied some men, and they rose and attempted to regain the battery. Wilcox's men held their ground "with a determination and courage unsurpassed." Officers and men engaged "in the most desperate personal conflicts with the enemy. The sword and bayonet were freely used." Charlie McNeill of Company D mounted one of the guns, waving the colors aloft, but was immediately shot. His nephew, William McNeill of A Company, tried to reach him but was killed before he could. Later, Charlie McNeil was found lying on the ground, pierced through the heart by a bayonet, and his flag was gone.[136]

One Confederate officer, Captain Walter Parker, felled two Union officers with his sword and then "was seriously wounded, receiving two bayonet wounds in the breast and one in his side and a musket wound breaking his left thigh."[137]

Lieutenant T.J. Michie of Company E was fighting man-to-man with a Union captain:

> *After receiving a ball from the captain's pistol in the right arm, a sword thrust in the cheek, and a cut which laid bare the skull bone on the crown of his head, Lieut. Mickey made a desperate thrust with his bright and flashing sword which penetrated and passed through the body of the gallant captain, who staggered back and in a moment fell a lifeless corpse.*

Michie fell, "cut over the head with a sabre-bayonet from behind, and afterward three bayonet wounds in the face and two in the breast…which he survived for three days." Soon the Federals troops attacked, and more bitter hand-to-hand combat ensued. "Few shots were fired…combatants stood breathless, face to face and foot to foot, with locked bayonets." Each man feared to release the lock "lest the other should gain the advantage." Officers climbed on the guns to rally their men, amid the storm of violence and death "unparalleled in the history of the rebellion." Randol rallied Company B of the 4th and some other scattered Federal troops, joined by the 7th Pennsylvania Reserves, and was able to drive the 11th Alabama back from the guns. Edmund DeWitt Patterson remembered that the fight "raged in all its fury around and above me—men ran over me, balls knocked dirt in my eyes." At any moment he feared that "a bullet might make my 'quietus' for me." As the 11th Alabama pulled back, "the great flag of some Pennsylvania regiment dragged across my face as I lay in the dust." The Alabamians continued to the wood line to the west, where they joined the 9th and 10th. Moving to the rear, William McIntosh of Company A took cover behind a tree. A Union soldier saw him and lunged at him with a bayonet, but "a puff of smoke from McIntosh's Enfield, and the Irishman's brains moistened the already crimson soil." Pennsylvanian Henderson Howard took on four Confederates, bayoneting two, shooting one and running the other off. Charles Shambaugh went to get his regiment's colors back. He struggled in among the mêlée and was able to grab the flagstaff. Returning to his own lines, he said, "I go-go-got the d-damned thing." The desperate fighting continued, but the Federal weight was beginning to tell. Failing to receive adequate support to hold the captured guns, Wilcox bitterly wrote, "It was a wrong inflicted upon that gallant little regiment to have left it unprotected at such a time." After driving Wilcox back, Randol saw even more Confederate troops approaching. The battle for the cannons was to continue. Neither side had the strength to hold the guns.[138]

A few days later, the wounded General Meade wrote a letter to Randol, summing up the situation very well:

> *I am aware, and shall so state, that everything that could be done by men similarly situated was done by yourself and command to repel the enemy and save your battery. I am also aware, and shall so state, that the loss of your battery was due to the failure of the infantry supports to maintain that firm and determined front which I should have expected from my men had not their morale been impaired by the fatigues incident to previous battles, constant marches, loss of rest and want of food, exhaustion their physical energies to such a degree that they were not able to withstand the desperate and determined onslaught of overwhelming numbers.*

Add to this the heat, terror and total confusion of the day, and it is amazing that the men of either side functioned as bravely as they did.[139]

During the desperate action, the common soldier was not the only one to become a casualty. The very competent Meade was trying to keep his men organized when he was hit with musket fire twice; one ball hit him in the forearm, and the other entered just above his hip and went out close to his spine. Unable to continue the fight, he rode to the rear. The Union had lost yet another field commander, one of its best.[140]

Chapter 11

Kearny Holds On

To the right of Randol was the division commanded by Phil Kearny. One of the Army of the Potomac's finest division commanders, Kearny was also one of its bravest—to a fault. He had fought with the French cavalry in the 1840s. In the American war with Mexico, he was wounded in his left arm, which had to be amputated. Following that conflict, Kearny returned to France and fought with the Imperial Guard of Emperor Napoleon III at Magenta and Solferino. Courage was something he demanded of his soldiers. General Winfield Scott called him "the bravest and most perfect soldier." Kearny hated cowardice, and perhaps most galling of all to him was the loss of an artillery piece during a fight.[141]

Kearny's division stretched from Randol's flank and reached out to touch Slocum's left at the Charles City Road. John Robinson's brigade was posted on the left, reaching out toward Meade. It was anchored by Thompson's battery. Robinson had the 63rd Pennsylvania on the left, the 57th Pennsylvania in the center and the 20th Indiana on his right. He kept the 105th Pennsylvania as his reserve. David Birney's brigade extended Robinson's flank to the Charles City Road, and Hiram Berry's brigade was held as a division reserve.[142]

Longstreet's string of uncoordinated attacks continued. Jenkins and Kemper had not attacked together, and Branch was late to support Kemper. Wilcox's attack was not well coordinated with Jenkins. Longstreet ordered Roger Pryor's brigade forward in support of Wilcox. Pryor's brigade consisted of the 14th Alabama, 2nd Florida, 1st Louisiana Battalion, 14th Louisiana and the 3rd Virginia. Although Pryor responded immediately, unfortunately for the Confederates the "wood and other obstructions" in front of his troops made movement difficult; he was forced to advance in column and send his regiments forward in succession rather than being able to mass an attack. The 14th Alabama went in first. As Pryor advanced toward Robinson's brigade, Wilcox's initial assault was being repulsed, so all available fire from the flank and the front was shifted to Pryor's men.[143]

Kearny wrote that Pryor's attack was launched with a "vigor and in such masses as I had never witnessed." It approached Lieutenant Pardon Jastram's section of Randolph's battery. Not very experienced, Jastram had trouble deciding where to fire. He also couldn't see to his front, as smoke covered the ground. Jastram received orders to "fire towards the sun." He ordered case shot with two-second fuses to be loaded, but one of his gunners loaded canister, which had to be fired in the air, as Jastram could not tell if his own troops were in his front. Adding to his troubles, he had only three men serving each piece. He fired through the blinding smoke and, after five rounds, noticed the men on his left (McCall's) pulling out. Soon the Federal troops to his front began falling back among his guns, and Jastram could no longer service them. He heard an officer shout for him to get his guns out. Fearing being captured, he decided to pull back but could not pull one of his cannons out, and it was spiked. Kearny would be contemptuous of Jastram's decision to withdraw his guns.[144]

Thompson's battery, however, was handled skillfully in defense. When Pryor's men were about 400 yards out, Thompson opened on them with spherical case shot. The Confederates "advanced in line, stooping down and firing." As they approached to within 150 yards, Thompson blasted them with double canister and "literally swept the slightly-falling open space with the completest execution." The attackers were mowed down by ranks and would pause momentarily, but soon they would be joined by supports and "increased masses came up and the wave bore on." Thompson's guns were tearing great gaps in the approaching line. When Thompson's canister supply was expended, he switched to cutting the fuses short on spherical case shot, which would cause the shells to explode almost immediately after being fired from the guns. This was extremely risky, as there was the great danger that the shells would explode prematurely, killing the crews serving the guns. Despite the risk, desperate times called for desperate measures. One shell took out half a dozen men of the 14th Louisiana. The 14th quickly lost 243 men of the 900 it began the attack with. One company entered the action with 42 men, but "only nine men came out without bullets in their hides." Pryor said that the 14th

New Jersey Brigade rushes to the aid of Kearny. *From* Frank Leslie's Illustrated History of the Civil War.

Alabama was "nearly annihilated." Even the innocent suffered: Pryor's horse became a casualty when its leg was blown off.[145]

In support, Colonel Alexander Hays advanced the 63rd Pennsylvania and the 37th New York Volunteers, and they blazed away at the approaching Confederates. Thompson told Hays that his guns were almost out of ammunition, and he needed help to cover the artillery. Hays ordered the 63rd Pennsylvania Volunteers forward. His men "sprang to their feet," advancing with bayonets. "The conflict was short, but most desperate, especially around the buildings of the R. Sykes farm. It was muzzle to muzzle, and the powder actually burned the faces of the opposing men."[146]

Kearny commended Hays's regiment, stating, "The Sixty-third has won for Pennsylvania the laurels of fame." The attackers who had survived the terror and carnage of the canister now faced the volleys of Hays's rifles. On Hays's right, the 20th Indiana "behaved with the greatest coolness… cracking jokes, loading and firing as if at a target." A member of that unit, A.J. Castater, said that General Kearny was sitting on his horse not 20 feet away," exhorting his men to not be afraid of the shelling—"just then a shell burst over us and a small piece of it hit the General in the breast without doing him any injury. He remarked that it was evident that the enemy would

"Kearny's Men" by Alfred Waud. *Courtesy of the Library of Congress.*

as soon hit a fellow as not, and rode down the line." The men of the 57th Pennsylvania fired as many as 150 rounds each, and John Robinson sent word to Berry to bring up reinforcements. His troops advanced in support, and the 2nd Michigan moved up to help the 20th Indiana. The 3rd Michigan went to support David Birney's brigade, on Robinson's right. The Confederates were temporarily repulsed but would not be denied so quickly. Thompson's gunners were firing so quickly that they did not take time to sponge the guns, increasing the slaughter but also raising the risk to his own crews.[147]

Thompson's guns finally expended all of their ammunition and withdrew from the field. He was able to pull five of his cannons and all of his caissons to safety. One gun was damaged and could not be pulled out, as some of its horses had been killed, so it was spiked and abandoned. In his report, Kearny lauded the performance of Thompson's battery for "the rapidity and precision of fire and coolness amid great loss of men and horses."[148]

Longstreet's final brigade, Winfield Featherson's undersized unit, consisted of the 12th and 19th Mississippi and the 2nd Mississippi Battalion. Arriving on Pryor's left, Featherston found himself on the extreme left end of the Confederate line. His men advanced to a fence, where they opened fire. The enemy returned "a well-directed fire" into his ranks, and

A.P. Hill. *Courtesy of the Library of Congress.*

Featherston sensed that they might attack his flank. Fearing that, he immediately sent word to Longstreet to send reinforcements. Having a small command (down to 250 men), he decided to wait for more troops. Featherston was soon hit in his shoulder and had to leave the field. All of Longstreet's troops had now been committed to battle. Without support from Huger on his left, he faced the possibility of being flanked by Kearny's division. A.P. Hill's division was sent in.[149]

Maxcy Gregg's brigade moved to the Confederate far left flank, and Gregg directed Colonel Samuel McGowan to form his lead regiment, the 14th South Carolina, and move forward through thick undergrowth to determine the position and strength of the enemy. He was heading toward Robinson's brigade of Kearny's division. Some of his men were sent ahead as skirmishers and, after advancing some three hundred yards, came upon the wounded Featherston, who warned them that the enemy was all around and that troops should be brought forward at once. McGowan ordered his regiment forward "through a perfect jungle of vines and bushes." They approached Federal skirmishers, who had been behind some hastily created breastworks and drove them off. He halted his regiment at a clearing and fired "volley after volley." The Federals of the 20th Indiana refused to retreat. They constructed a makeshift breastwork of logs and fence rails and returned "a very hot and fatal fire." Having picked up extra cartridges, some of McGowan's men fired as many as seventy rounds. McGowan remembered that after dark the firing slowed, and enemy officer approached the lines, asking what unit they were. He then demanded to know what unit the officer was from, to which was replied the 20th Indiana. The Confederate colonel replied that they were from the 14th South Carolina and had the Federal officer escorted to the rear. In a few moments, they heard a command from across the field: "Commence firing!" The line blazed. The Federals "poured into the regiment for a short time the most destructive fire. We, however, held our ground and returned the fire until the enemy fled." The Union troops made one attempt to turn Gregg's flank, but Lieutenant Colonel Simpson directed fire at them and pushed the attackers back. The shooting continued for some time until it finally faded out. Gregg's 13th South Carolina was beside the 14th but could not fire safely owing to the terrain and general confusion. The men fixed bayonets and prepared to attack but never received that order.[150]

At about 7:30 p.m., Kearny grew concerned about his far right, near the Charles City Road. Feeling comfortable that his left and center would hold, Kearny rode to his flank and saw that only the "weak Third Michigan" was in reserve. However, he soon noticed the "cheerful manner and solid look" of Birney's brigade. Warning them of the threat, "they met my warning of the coming storm with loud cheers of exultation." Kearny spent thirty or forty minutes on this excursion, returning to the far left of his line. He found that Colonel Francis Barlow's 239-man regiment of the 61st New York volunteers had come up. Barlow was from Caldwell's brigade of Sumner's division. Barlow's men had become separated from the brigade as they marched toward the sound of the guns. Arriving on the field, Barlow was directed by General Robinson to form his men on the border of a large field and behind a fence. Ordered to advance into the field, they fixed bayonets, climbed over the fence and advanced into the open field. His men soon picked up a Confederate flag that had the inscriptions "Seven Pines and

Fair Oaks" on it. They continued to push across the field to the wood line, where they opened fire that was "vigorously returned." Barlow's men soon approached the woods on the other side of the field.[151]

Between the gathering darkness and the smoke, sight was becoming difficult. Making out a group of men on the other side of the field, Confederates asked what regiment Barlow's troops belonged to. When they responded "61st New York," the reply was, "Throw down your arms, or you are all dead men." The New Yorkers opened fire. Caldwell sent the 81st Pennsylvania Volunteers in to relieve the New Yorkers, but both regiments

Phil Kearny. *Courtesy of the Library of Congress.*

continued firing until they had exhausted their ammunition. Concerned that the enemy was about to strike his left flank, Barlow moved the two regiments to a parapet on the right of the field. Temporarily withdrawn by Caldwell, Barlow's group was later ordered to occupy the parapet by Kearny. It would spend the night there.[152]

Heintzelman received a call for aid from Kearny and sent the New Jersey Brigade from Slocum's division, Kearny's old command, plus a battery of guns. Because of Huger's inaction, men could be pulled from Slocum's front. Riding along, Kearny soon saw that McCall's division had "abandoned" its position, and he sent the 1st New Jersey Brigade under the "true hands" of Brigadier General George Taylor to fill the gap. Legend has it that Kearny unwittingly rode into a group of Confederates. In the smoke and confusion, an officer rode up to Kearny and asked, "My men are in position sir, what shall I do?" Kearny responded, "Do as I have always directed you to do in such a situation, you fool!" and then turned and quickly rode away. Under severe pressure, Kearny's line had held, but at a great cost.[153]

Chapter 12

THE FINAL ACTIONS

Night was now approaching. Longstreet still hoped that Huger and Jackson would appear and sent orders for Magruder to march back up from the New Market Road area. The weight of Magruder's command might have tipped the scales in favor of the Confederates at this moment, but instead, it was wasted by marching and countermarching all day. Meanwhile, it was the Federals who were sending in fresh troops, heading for the location of Cooper's and Randol's guns. On the Confederate left, Featherston was in danger of being flanked by the influx of Northern reinforcements. More importantly, these units threatened Longstreet's entire line. With his men exhausted and the opportunity for the real victory slipping away, Longstreet could wait no longer and ordered A.P. Hill to send in his remaining brigades. Charles Field's Virginians were the first to go in, moving through the spent troops of Jenkins and Wilcox. Dorsey Pender and James Archer would follow, and Joseph Reid Anderson's brigade was to be held in reserve.[154]

Field, in response to orders to enter the action "as soon as possible," had his column advance at the double-quick and then move into attacking formation up both sides of the Long Bridge Road, with the 55th and 60th Virginia on the right side and the 47th Virginia, along with the 2nd Virginia Battalion, on the left. The 40th Virginia had become separated from the others by the terrain, so it was farther to the left, heading toward Francis Barlow's attack. Field had learned that the guns to his front had been taken and retaken in a seesaw battle. About three hundred yards ahead, he saw Cooper's and Randol's batteries, each of which had changed hands several

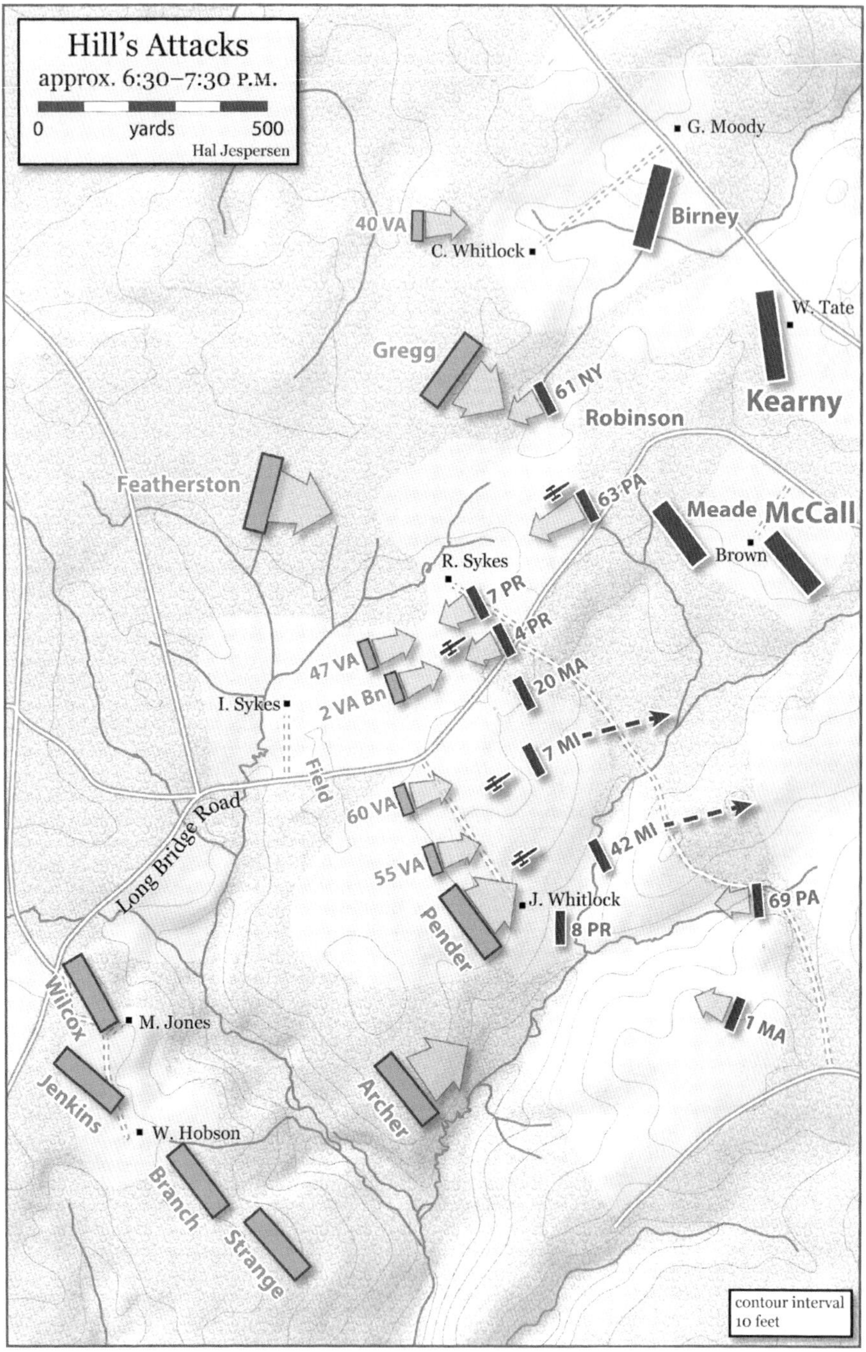

"Hill's Attacks." *Map by Hal Jespersen.*

times during the afternoon and which were currently held by the Federals, who could not pull them out owing to the loss of so many horses.[155]

As soon as Field's men were close enough, they attacked. Field said, "The charge was impetuously made, and was an instance where bayonets were really crossed." His reserved tone does not do justice to the terror of a bayonet fight. As the Confederates approached, the Northern artillerymen fired as fast as they could, blasting great holes in the attackers' lines. Defenders fought with clubbed muskets, bayonets and even ramrods in a desperate attempt to hold the guns. Field's men gathered themselves, and in a rush, his men captured Randol's battery. One of the defenders desperately pulled the lanyard of one of the guns but fired over the heads of Field's Virginians. As the Federals abandoned the guns, the 47th turned one of the guns on them, which aided Gregg, currently fighting on the left flank. The Federals had to pull out, abandoning Randol's guns one final time. The Confederates had finally captured them for good.[156]

Although separated from the rest of the brigade, the 40th Virginia had a fight of its own. A large body of Federal troops approached the men. Driving them back, Sergeant Vincent Branson exclaimed, "Now Colonel, let's give them the bayonet!" He was immediately hit by a Yankee bullet and fell. From sheer exhaustion, the men dropped where they were.[157]

Men of the 7th Pennsylvania Reserves fired at Field's brigade as the Confederates advanced, but attackers continued forward deliberately. The desperate fight of bayonets and clubbed muskets continued. The scene was terrible, made up of desperate, individual attempts at survival. Wounded men lay all over the ground, often being trampled by other soldiers. Lifeless men began to pile up. Dead horses were everywhere. Private Benjamin Early of the 7th Pennsylvania Reserves saved Colonel Henry Bolinger's life by ramming his bayonet into a Confederate soldier just below his armpit. Unable to stem the Confederate tide, the 7th pulled back, joining up with several other regiments in the rear. The Confederates finally had to stop. Colonel Robert Mayo, commander of the 47th Virginia, said that he had a force of a about three hundred men. He pulled up to wait for reinforcements as darkness approached.[158]

On Field's right, the 55th and 60th Virginia advanced at the double-quick toward Cooper's battery. The 55th, under Colonel Francis Mallory, was to the right; the 60th was to its left. As the 55th advanced and could see over the hill, it saw Cooper's abandoned guns "the brigade which had taken it had disappeared and the enemy had advanced to within a few yards of the battery." Mallory's men pulled up, fired several volleys and then charged, driving the enemy back into the woods. Fearing being flanked, they fell back to the edge of the woods and remained.[159]

Like the 55th, the 60th marched over the brow of the hill and then fired several volleys into the defenders. Led by Colonel William E. Starke, they charged, drove the Federals back into the woods and followed them for "a considerable distance." The defenders "poured a heavy fire into our line, upon which the command was given to charge bayonets." The fighting was desperate, as it was in so many places this day. Private Robert A. Christian, called the "Father of the Regiment" because he had enlisted at almost sixty years of age, had displayed admirable "energy" and "patriotism" and was thought of highly by the men of the regiment. Christian was attacked "by no less than four of the enemy. He killed three of his assailants with his own hands while being wounded by several bayonet thrusts." His brother Eli rushed to his aid and killed the fourth attacker. Due to wounds and illness, commands of companies were falling to lieutenants. One of them, I.H. Larew of Company E, earned his colonel's praise by seizing his company's colors and carrying them boldly in front of his regiment until the enemy was driven off. Starke's men continued to drive the defenders further but soon had to halt, as "it being then quite dark."[160]

William Dorsey Pender's brigade advanced down the Long Bridge Road, with Field quite some distance ahead and on his left. He ran into some Federal troops who were between him and Field, charging from right to left at the double-quick, and who apparently did not see Pender. They were about seventy-five yards in front when Pender's men promptly attacked and scattered them, driving into the woods. In front of the Confederates was an abandoned battery, and Federal troops were on the right. These made several efforts at Pender's force. He was able to repel them and drive into the woods, but the Federals were able to pull the guns out. With darkness approaching, low on ammunition and hearing from the prisoners they had taken that there was a strong enemy force ahead, Pender pulled back and held some of the ground his men had taken. James Archer advanced on his right flank, providing much-needed support.[161]

The Pennsylvania Reserves had received the most vicious parts of the Confederate attack. After three days of battle during the past five days, they were badly mauled. All of the brigade commanders were out of action. Simmons was killed, and Meade had been wounded. Seymour had wandered off, ostensibly searching for help. Successive waves of Confederate attacks had decimated them, regiment by regiment. The remains of the division attempted to re-form in the rear as a sort of brigade. It was dark, and the

Abandoned Union batteries by Henry Clow. *Courtesy of the County of Henrico, Virginia Historic Preservation and Museum Services.*

men were exhausted; not much more could be done that day. Many of the men of the reserves had fought as bravely as anyone during the actions of the past week. Around 10:00 p.m., Seymour returned and took over leadership, and at about 11:00 p.m., they received orders to pull out in the direction of Malvern Hill.[162]

Darkness was settling in, and Hill was concerned about the arrival of more Federal reinforcements. Two brigades from Richardson's division of the Second Corps and one from Slocum's division of the Sixth Corps were arriving to back up Kearny. Hill had but one brigade remaining in reserve, that of Joseph Reid Anderson. Anderson was the owner of the Tredegar Iron Works in Richmond, the Confederacy's most important industrial plant. A West Point graduate, he had been assigned a brigade in Hill's Light Division. After the battle, he and Lee would agree that he would be of greatest service back at the factory, keeping the Confederacy's war machine running. On this day, however, he was Hill's last chance.[163]

Anderson received orders from Hill to advance. He moved forward, the Long Bridge Road dividing his force. The 3rd Louisiana Battalion and the 14th Georgia were to the left. Across the road, to their right, were the 35th, 45th and 49th Georgia. Lieutenant Colonel Pendleton of the 3rd Louisiana was ordered to lead the left wing, and Anderson would command the right. At this moment, President Davis arrived on the scene, galloping the entire length of the line, and was "vociferously cheered by the men." It was now sunset. Hill ordered the left wing to advance first, and he then instructed Anderson to take the right wing forward. Hill warned that a brigade of Confederates was to their front. In the twilight, Anderson instructed that no muskets were to be fired until they recognized who was in front of them. Justifiably, he was concerned that they might open fire on friends. They marched about half a mile, with "the sound and flash of the musketry indicating the enemy's position on the left of the road." Anderson shifted his men to the left into a position that was roughly in front of the enemy. By the time he completed this movement, night had fallen.[164]

Soon Anderson's wing came upon a force "which seemed to be a brigade or division" approaching and was convinced that they were the enemy. At a distance of fifty to seventy-five yards, the approaching men yelled, "For God's sake, don't fire on us; we are friends." Not wanting to fire but trying to determine if they were friend or foe, Anderson ordered his men to a bayonet charge at the double-quick. "All doubt should have been removed by the command of 'fire' on the part of the enemy." The left wing, particularly the 45th Georgia, took the brunt of the fire. He ordered his men to lie down and keep up a steady fire. This they did, until the Federals pulled back. Among the casualties was Colonel Thomas Hardeman of the 45th and Anderson himself, who was hit in the head by a spent ball. Command fell to Colonel Edward L. Thomas.[165]

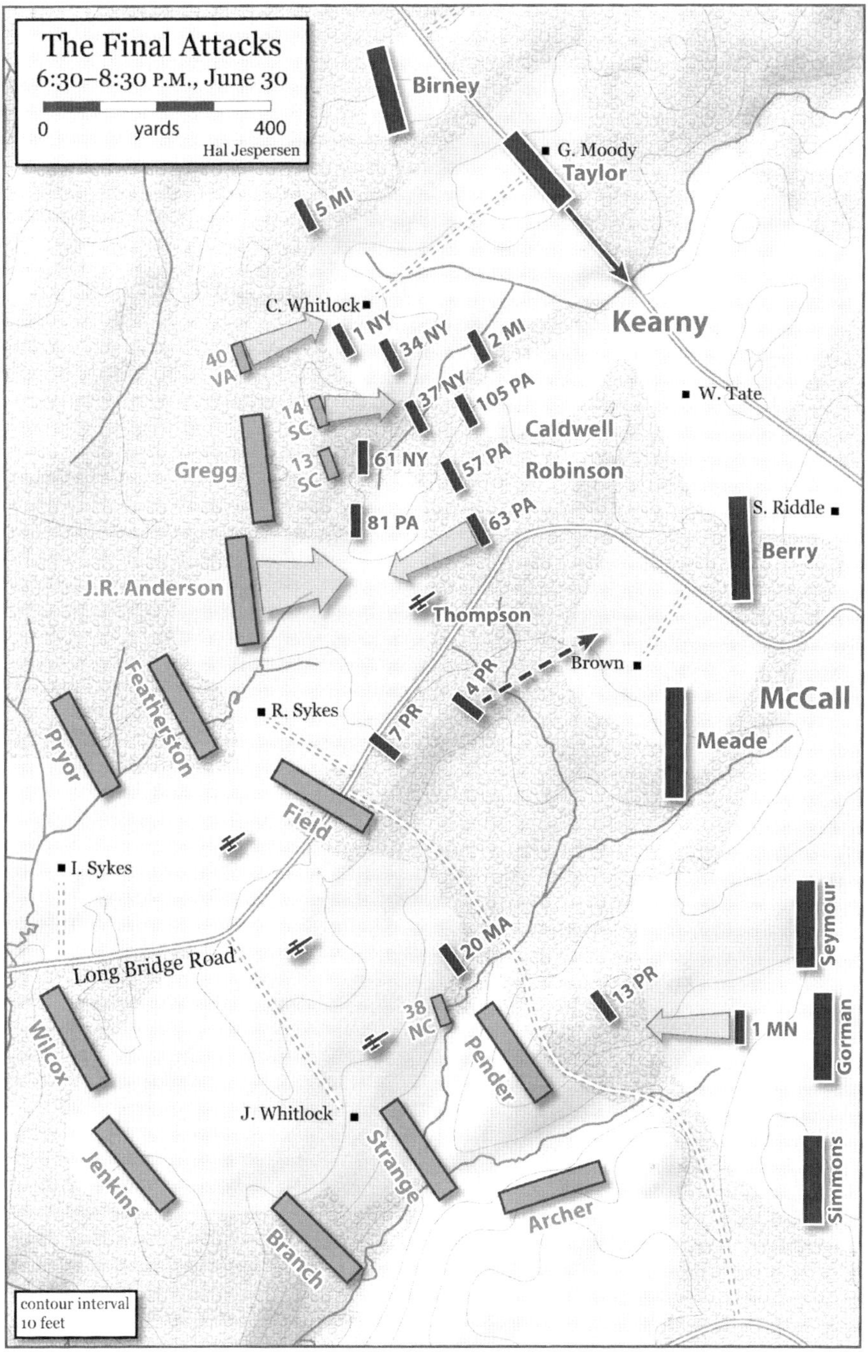

"The Final Attacks." *Map by Hal Jespersen.*

In the darkness, the firing became confined to the right of what remained of McCall's position and "was becoming slack and interrupted." Lieutenant Colonel William Thompson rode up to McCall and said that he had pulled together about five hundred men, with whom he was then advancing. McCall rode up the road with him, trying to connect with Kearny. He took three men and rode forward to reconnoiter the situation. After riding about one hundred yards, he ran directly into the 47th Virginia. In the darkness, he had not seen them, as they were positioned under some trees. One of the men inquired who the men in the trees were, and Colonel Mayo of the 47th yelled at the top of his voice, "Friends!" Someone on the left called out, "47th Virginia!," and two of the riders attempted to sprint away. McCall turned to escape, but a soldier, Brooke Rollins, grabbed his horse's rein and said, "Not so fast." McCall and a courier were immediately taken prisoner. The general was taken to Longstreet, and General Lee happened to be present. Longstreet had served with McCall in the old 4th Infantry and offered his hand as McCall dismounted. Longstreet remembered, "I saw that he did not regard the occasion as one for renewing old friendship, and I merely offered him some of my staff as an escort to Richmond."[166]

As night fell, the furious sound of battle gradually faded. Attempts to continue the action in the dark were futile; friend could not be discerned from foe. Under the cover of darkness, the Federal army pulled out, continuing its retreat toward the James. Moving down Willis Church Road, it gathered itself behind the strong position established by Fitz John Porter and the artillery of Henry Hunt.

After the violent and terrible day, all that was left were the screams and moans of the wounded and the silence of the dead. The "wailing of the wounded blended into one blood-chilling cry of pain." One of the last to leave the field, Joseph Hooker recalled the scene: "From the torches we could see that the enemy was busy all night long in searching for his wounded, but up to daylight the following morning there had been no apparent diminution in the heart-rending cries and groans of his wounded. The unbroken, mournful wail of human suffering was all that we heard from Glendale during that long, dismal night."[167]

Chapter 13

AFTERMATH

Willis Church was quite old when the armies arrived. The Methodists had received the land in 1803 and built the wooden church shortly thereafter. Intended to be a peaceful place of reflection and worship, instead it was to become the center of horror after the battle. Dr. H.G. Taylor of the 8th New Jersey said that they "immediately commenced to remove all the pews, in order to make room for the accommodation of the wounded." As the wounded "poured in upon us," the building soon was full. Many had to be moved outside. The medical staff gave both sides equal attention. "By dark…we had over 200 wounded at the church and although there were 18 surgeons, it was nearly 2 o'clock before we lay down." Dr. Benjamin Roher of the 10th Pennsylvania Reserves remembered, "The shells fell all about us while in the church, yet we all escaped." He said, "Arms & legs were piled up…in one corner of the church, terrible to behold."[168]

A soldier of the 7th New York remembered that night: "The few hours I spent here are the most disagreeable and despair of my life. Think of half starved men, the few clothes we wear, soaked with persperation, grime and powdersmoke, and yet so cold that our teeth were chattering, burning thirsts and dry throats and toungs. A kingdom for a piece of bread and a drink of water!"[169]

As the day ended, more and more animals were added to the rolls of the dead. Robert Knox Sneden said, "A large number of lame and wounded horses and mules were to be killed to prevent them falling into the enemy's hands. I followed and soon saw the poor animals slaughtered by

Willis Church. *Author's collection.*

lance and pistol." He estimated that there were about 230 killed in this manner.[170]

Federal troops were ordered to pull out during the night and headed for the shelter of Malvern Hill and the Federal gunboats in the river beyond. They had fought tenaciously to hold their ground—now they were giving it up. Worse, they had to leave many of their wounded comrades behind to the mercy of the Confederates. The men were exhausted and hungry. It was a very hard night for them.

The Nelson house was surrounded by Confederate troops, and both Confederate and Federal wounded were being attended. A Federal later wrote, "There were very few complaints amongst our men…they mentioned with gratitude many acts of kindness." It was that kind of war. Violent efforts to kill and maim would often be followed by mercy and compassion when the fighting stopped. For some, the end of the fighting was eternal. A Federal veteran later said that "there were ten or more lying side by side. The dew had fallen heavily on their faces, and the light of the rising sun glittered on their brows like gems."[171]

The next morning presented a terrible scene to the Confederates:

> *Yonder stood those grim guns; yonder lay the dead from the Federal infantry supports, behind improvised breastworks of rails, sods, anything, however frail, that promised protection from the leaden hail. On the right of these guns stood a small cabin, literally honey-combed by shot. Around in ghastly heaps lay the dead more of gray, alas, than blue! Gallant fellows! How could they stem that torrent of flame and capture those guns, whose grim mouths were black from hurling death!*

Grave in the Willis Church yard. *Author's collection.*

The same soldier wrote of a mother returning to the field, holding her child: "She stood gazing upon the bloody scene."[172]

By nightfall, Longstreet's and A.P. Hill's divisions had failed to break through and seize the Willis Church Road. Both sides had fought desperately, with men displaying incredible bravery and devotion. Yet when all was done, both sides were roughly in the same positions as they had been when the day began. McClellan was able to complete his escape; his army would not be cut in two and would survive to fight another day. Why had the Confederate effort failed? What were the costs of this long and miserable day? What would be the repercussions?

While not the bloodiest of the Seven Days Battles (Gaines's Mill would claim that distinction), the results of the action at Frayser's Farm were nonetheless horrific. Exact totals are impossible to know for certain, but total losses range from 6,300 to 7,400 killed, wounded and missing for both sides, out of 42,700 troops involved. This equates to casualties of between 14.75 and 17.3 percent.

CONFEDERATE

Porter Alexander estimated Longstreet's losses at 2,600, killed, wounded and missing. He said that A.P. Hill suffered about 1,700 casualties, for a total Confederate loss of 4,300. Other estimates vary slightly. Brian Burton placed the Confederate casualties at about 3,500, and Louis Manarin estimated them at 3,615. Leon Tenney calculated 3,573. Some of the regimental losses were appalling. Micah Jenkins's Palmetto Sharpshooters suffered 39 killed and 215 wounded out of 375 men, a 67 percent loss. The 11th Alabama had 49 killed and 121 wounded, a 50 percent casualty rate.[173]

James Kemper reported his brigade's loss at 44 killed, 205 wounded and 165 missing, for a total of 414 men. Branch stated that he suffered 800 casualties. In his report, Wilcox lamented his loss of 471 men; Strange claimed a loss of 228 out of 728 available.[174]

Whatever the precise totals were, the losses were severe for the two divisions involved. For their efforts, the Confederates captured fourteen guns, some small arms and Union general George McCall. Of greater importance, the Union army escaped intact to fight another day.

UNION

It was also a bloody day for the Federals. Brian Burton estimates their losses at 2,800 killed, wounded and missing. Louis Manarin wrote that the Federal casualties were 2,853. Uzal Ent agrees closely with Manarin, citing *Fox' Regiments*: 210 dead, 1,515 wounded and 1,130 missing, giving a total of

2,855. Leon Tenney, in his study of the losses of the Seven Days Campaign, estimated 2,935. William Powell, in his comprehensive history of the Fifth Corps, said that McCall's division lost 1,113. This was out of a unit that had already been reduced to 6,000 men after its actions at Beaver Dam Creek and Gaines's Mill.[175]

There were recriminations on the Federal side. In his report of July 15, Hooker said, "The whole of McCall's division was completely routed," with fugitives running through and disrupting his lines, some who "actually fired on and killed some of my men as they passed." An exchange of letters ensued, with McCall being defended by a number of commanders from the Pennsylvania Reserves. Hooker held firm to his position, but in one letter he did state that McCall's command "nobly redeemed themselves at South Mountain and Antietam." It is doubtful that this was enough to remove any strain from their relationship. Longstreet later said of McCall, "He was more tenacious of his battle than any one who came within my experience during the war, if I except D.H. Hill at Sharpsburg."[176]

Of the day, McClellan (who was not there) wrote to Edwin Stanton, "Another day of desperate fighting. We are pressed by superior numbers." As was typical, he continued, "I fear I shall be forced to abandon my material and the cover of the Gun Boats. You must send us very large reinforcements." The patience of forceful commanders like Hooker and Kearny was wearing thin. The day following the battle at Malvern Hill, McClellan was to order a retreat to the safety of the Federal gunboats. A soldier in the 1st New Jersey remarked on McClellan's absence, "He had withdrawn himself from the immediate vicinity of the battle-field where, had the consequences been averse, his army would have been lost." Of McClellan's lack of aggressiveness, Kearny was to say that McClellan's actions were "prompted by cowardice or treason." These were harsh words, but McClellan had taken his magnificent army and surrendered the initiative to his opponent. In the end, it was the leadership of corps, division and brigade commanders that saved the Union army from a potential disaster.[177]

In the end, the Federals had escaped. Lee's trap had failed to close. His plan should have worked; Lee seemed to have his men in the right place at the right time. The Federal troops were strung out, somewhat haphazardly, sometimes not even connected to one another. They were tired after fighting days of consecutive battles, followed by nights of exhausting marching. Their commander was nowhere to be found; instead, he was on board the *Galena* in the James River. Despite these disadvantages, the Federals enjoyed some very good fortune this day. Although their forces were strung out in long retreat, three of their best fighters just happened to be in perfect position when Longstreet attacked. Phil Kearny, who had a solid reputation as an experienced and aggressive battlefield commander, was on the right. "Fighting Joe" Hooker was on the left, and George Gordon Meade, the future commander of the Army of the Potomac, was a brigade commander under McCall in the center. Luck could hardly have better blessed the Federal army.

Everything seemed to be lined up for Lee. Huger was nearly in position to launch the day's battle by attacking the Federal center on Charles City Road. Holmes was at the end of the line, near the river, apparently ready to strike at the head of the Federal column and possibly seize Malvern Hill, the dominant topographical position. Magruder's command, tired after its limited action at Savage's Station, was in reserve behind Longstreet and A.P. Hill. Their combined force should have been able to strike toward the crossroads and seize the Federals' route of escape, the Willis Church Road. Finally, Stonewall Jackson, the fearless and aggressive leader of the Valley army, would pounce on the Union rear guard at White Oak Swamp. If all went according to plan, at least half of the Army of the Potomac would be cut off. Perhaps the entire army would be destroyed. Were that to happen, what would be the resulting outcome on the course of the war? Would the Federals continue the fight with the core of troops stationed near Fredericksburg, or would there be a call to negotiate? Answers to these questions will never be known.

For Lee, almost nothing went right. While fortune smiled on the army in blue, it seemed to completely abandon the Confederates. Huger did not launch the keynote attack. Instead, he was bogged down removing trees and cutting a new road. His total lack of aggressiveness cost the Confederates heavily that day, and it would cost him personally. Holmes, down by the river, accomplished nothing. Union general Fitz John Porter seized and fortified Malvern Hill, leaving Holmes's force as barely a distraction. John Bankhead Magruder, who was to provide a reserve for the main Confederate attack of Longstreet and Hill, instead was sent down to the river to support Holmes; then, after the issue in the center was already decided, he was recalled. The action at Frayser's Farm became a battle of reinforcements. When the Confederates drove McCall from the center and had the greatest opportunity to seize the Willis Church Road, the Federals were able to pull men from Huger's inactive front and from the White Oak area. These troops arrived in time and saved the Union route of retreat. Were Magruder's men in place backing Longstreet and Hill, it is conceivable that they could have given the Confederates enough force to seize and hold the road. Sadly for the Confederacy, Magruder accomplished nothing that day, although he can hardly be blamed.

The greatest disappointment, of course, was the behavior of Stonewall Jackson. The legendary leader of the astonishing Confederate victories in the Shenandoah Valley, Jackson continued the dilatory performance he had exhibited so far in the outskirts of Richmond. This was probably the nadir of his career, and the timing could not have been worse. He had failed to strike a blow at Franklin, who was commanding the tail of the Federal army. He had not examined opportunities to cross where Hampton had suggested and had not checked out the crossing at Brackett's. Either might have placed him on one of Franklin's flanks. Brackett's would have also placed him on Slocum's flank. Not only did he fail to damage the Federals before him, but his inactivity also allowed troops to be pulled from his sector and sent to the Glendale area just in time to shore up the Federal defenses that were crumbling.

Longstreet, who was one of the few generals following Lee's plan, had problems of his own. His attacks were disjointed, with Kemper's men rushing out in front of other units, and Micah Jenkins, Branch, Strange, Wilcox, Featherston and Pryor were unable to attack in unison. Instead of having the division attack as one, each brigade's attack was made on its own, allowing the defenders to shift troops to meet different threats. This scenario would repeat itself, on a larger scale, in the Union actions at Antietam a little over two months later. While there were reasons for each failure to coordinate, the effective power of one massed attack on McCall's division was lost. Add to this the failures of Huger, Holmes and Jackson, and the wasted day of marching Magruder's troops back and forth, and the Confederates had a recipe for failure, if not disaster. It was a testament to the bravery and hard fighting of the troops who did attack that they were able to come even remotely close to their goal. One other thing stood in Lee's way, and its importance cannot be minimized: the bravery and determination of the Federal soldiers who opposed him.

If these weren't problems enough, Lee had even more. His army was new, especially to him. He had a small, inexperienced staff, not big enough to control an army that was so large and dispersed. The staff officers were also new to him and were unfamiliar with his methods. Lee's standard mode of operation was to draw up his plan, communicate it to his subordinates and then let them work out the details and execute it. He relied heavily on his commanders' ability to carry out his orders. On this day, Lee had four commanders who were not performing up to expectation (Huger, Holmes, Magruder and Jackson). He would have been much better if he had an experienced staff to keep an eye on each segment of the battle and ensure that his orders were followed. Lee did not have the reach to monitor each of his subordinates' performance, nor did he attempt to. As a result, his plans were not carried out. Alexander later commented, "An army is like a great machine, and in putting it into battle it is not enough for its commander to merely issue the necessary orders. He should have a staff ample to supervise the execution of each step & to promptly report any difficulty or misunderstanding." This shortcoming was crucial.[178]

The Army of Northern Virginia was not yet organized into corps, unlike its Union counterpart. This forced Lee to have direct command of a large number of subordinates, which was unwieldy. The staff issues compounded the problem. It would prove to be more effective to have direct command of only two or three. Lee would soon remedy this situation.

Another problem for his army was the poor quality of the maps available of the outskirts of Richmond. Lee had been stationed with the high command in Richmond. He was an excellent engineer, but little had been done in the way of producing accurate maps prior to June 1862. When Lee took command of the army, he made the creation of maps a priority. Unfortunately, much of the land the army would need maps of was, at that time, behind Union lines. Maps could not be created in time, so reliance would have to be placed on some sketched maps that were not wholly accurate, as well as the guidance of locals.[179]

After the end of the campaign, Lee took quick action to remove what he considered weaknesses in his higher command. Huger was sent away. Holmes and Magruder were banished to the Trans-Mississippi. Holmes and Huger were totally ineffective; Lee was right to move them out. At first, it might seem unfair that Magruder was replaced. He had bad luck at Savage's Station and was completely mishandled at Glendale. The next day, he would come under fire for beginning the ill-fated attack on Malvern Hill, but it is questionable that he deserved all of the blame. Where Lee was perceptive, and correct, was that Magruder was too excitable to handle the responsibility that would be required of him. The most interesting decision involved Stonewall Jackson. He had been no less a failure than the others and was a greater disappointment. Lee, however, had seen the flashes of brilliance in the Valley. Fortunately for the Confederacy, Lee very wisely took no action against Jackson. This would prove to be one of Lee's greatest decisions.

Some saw their reputations enhanced. Longstreet and Hill came out of the battle appearing to be solid and aggressive combat commanders. Wilcox and Jenkins were also aggressive. Realizing that he needed to have better control of his army and enhanced coordination of their actions, Lee decided to reorganize it. The Confederate government had not authorized a structure that included corps (a corps is a group of two or more divisions placed under one overall commander). Getting around this limitation, Lee proceeded to form two "wings." One would be under James Longstreet, and interestingly, if not presciently, he assigned the other wing to Jackson. The army would achieve great results under this structure and with these two commanders.

In the end, it was a day of great disappointment for Lee's army and for the Confederacy. Remarkable victories were to follow and the legend of the Army of Northern Virginia would be born, but one of the South's greatest opportunities had eluded it. Would it ever be this strong again, and would it ever have such an opportunity? Lee's early biographer, Douglas Southall Freeman, noted:

> *It was the bitterest disappointment that Lee had ever sustained, and one that he could not conceal. Many times thereafter he was to discover a weak point in his adversary's line or a mistake in his antagonist's plan, but never again was he to find the enemy in full retreat across his front. Victories in the field were to be registered, but two years of open campaign were not to produce another situation where envelopment seemed possible. He had only that one day for a Cannae, and his army was not ready for it.*

Despite the disappointment, the Federal threat had been driven from the gates of Richmond, and as one Confederate soldier remarked, "One thing it has accomplished, it has imbued every man of ours with a determination to fight like demons." Cadmus Wilcox said, "Had the orders of the Confederate Commander been carried out as contemplated…[it] would have been most disastrous, in all probability, to the Federals." As for Union cause, General Phil Kearney noted that the battle was "one of the most desperate of the war, the one most fatal if lost."[180]

Thinking of Lee, Porter Alexander summed it up: "I have often thought that in his retrospect of the war no one day of the whole four years would seem to him more unfortunate than June 30, 1862. It was, undoubtedly, the opportunity of his life, for the Confederacy was then in its prime, with more men available than ever before or after. And at no other period would the moral or the physical effect of a victory have been so great as upon this occasion."[181]

It was a great tragedy for the Confederacy and a fortunate day for the Union. The immediate struggle, however, was not over; it would be played out in violence and blood the next day on the gentle slope of Malvern Hill.

Appendix I

FLAG OF THE 11TH ALABAMA

To paraphrase Robert E.L. Krick, historian of the Richmond National Battlefield Park, one of the most compelling things about Civil War battlefields is to take human-interest stories and attach them to the ground where they happened. This is indeed the case with the flag of the 11th Alabama. On June 27, at Gaines's Mill, Cadmus Wilcox attacked the left of the Union Fifth Corps in Lee's attempt to break the enemy's line and crush the portion of Federal army north of the Chickahominy.

Near the climax of the battle, Wilcox's brigade crossed Boatswain's Creek to attack the Union defenders on the opposing ridge. The first person to carry the flag of the 11th was a man named Maxwell, who upon first appearing in front of the enemy was riddled with thirteen bullets and killed. The next soldier to pick it up was a teenage farmer named Danbury Jones, who grabbed the flag and led the charge across the creek. He was hit first in the arm, which was broken by the impact of the bullet. Soon he was hit in both legs and then in the other arm. The flag was taken from him, but Jones protested. He said that although he was shot in both legs, he could still walk, and as for his arms, he asked that the flagpole be tied to his body. This was not done, and the regiment swept by on its way to routing the Union defenders.

However, this wasn't the end of the flag's story. Just three days later, it was present in another desperate struggle at Frayser's Farm. Charlie McNeill was the flag bearer. As the 11th stormed Alanson Randol's guns, McNeill carried the flag into the fray and was mortally wounded. His nephew Billy came to his rescue (and the flag's) and was killed. After the battle, members of the 11th found Charlie's body, which had been bayoneted through the heart. The 11th's colors were gone.

In 1906, the flag was given to the Museum of the Confederacy in Richmond, where it has been conserved and is now part of its amazing flag collection. The story of the flag can be found online at https://www.youtube.com/watch?v=MomD5mf-rug, or more simply, go to YouTube and enter "Battle of Glendale."

Appendix II

Glendale Today

It had been so frustrating. Until the late 1990s, one could drive by the Glendale battlefield but couldn't visit it. Nearly all the land was in private hands. The National Park Service had 1 acre total, more or less, across from the national cemetery, but otherwise the site appeared to be gone forever. It seemed tragic that such an important place could be so irretrievably lost. All that began to change during the 1990s when the Association for the Preservation of Civil War Sites (the precursor to the Civil War Trust) was able to purchase the southern tip of the battlefield. Amazingly, in the next few years, the trust saved 619 acres (most of the battlefield). By 2013, 394 acres had been turned over to the park. This was unprecedented in Civil War preservation. Robert E.L. Krick, historian for the Richmond National Battlefield Park, said that "there has been nothing like it before in Virginia... never before in modern times has anyone preserved a battlefield virtually from scratch." This was the intriguing thing about studying this battle. Heavily wooded, the land is pristine, with few signs or markers. It is nearly a virgin site.

In its August 12, 2013 press release, the Civil War Trust remarked, "Several generations of local families were responsible stewards of a large part of the battlefield. Their commitment to the integrity of the landscape made the land still worth saving." One of those landowners, Dr. Len Morrow, told the trust, "When you think of all the folks who died there, some at the point of a bayonet...that's a sobering experience to contemplate." Landowners worked with the trust, and with the contributions of its fifty thousand members,

View from the Glendale Visitor Center. *Courtesy of Ashley Luskey.*

funds were raised and an endangered battlefield has been saved. Much of the land is now in the possession of the National Park Service. Within a few years, walking trails should be in place, and people will be able to understand and appreciate what happened on this hallowed ground.[182]

It bears mentioning that the Civil War Trust, and its local colleagues in the Richmond Battlefields Association, have been very active throughout the Richmond area. In addition to the acquisitions made at Glendale, almost all of nearby Malvern Hill has been saved. Land has been purchased at Cold Harbor, and a very large tract, along with some smaller parcels, has been acquired at Gaines's Mill. A significant portion of the North Anna battlefield was saved. Future generations will owe a great deal to these organizations and their members.

Appendix III

After the Battle

The Leaders

Confederate

Joseph Reid Anderson

While Anderson returned to active duty following his wounding, he promptly resigned and was soon back at work directing the operations at the Tredegar Iron Works. The factory was the most important producer of cannons and munitions for the Southern war effort, and Anderson's leadership was invaluable. He helped the operation survive the war, continued to manage it during the postwar years and was followed by his son Archer. Anderson died on September 7, 1892, and is buried at Hollywood Cemetery in Richmond, Virginia.[183]

Lawrence O'Bryan Branch

Following the Peninsula Campaign, Branch was with A.P. Hill's division at Cedar Mountain and contributed to the Confederate victory. He was on the Confederate far left at Second Manassas and was a brigade commander with Hill as the latter's division saved the day for the Southerners at Antietam (Sharpsburg). At the southern end of that field, Branch was hit in the cheek by a bullet and died instantly. He is buried at Old City Cemetery in Raleigh, North Carolina.[184]

Ambrose Powell Hill

In July 1862, Hill was assigned to Jackson's command and played a key role in the battle at Cedar Mountain. He ran afoul of Jackson, who placed him under arrest before the army crossed into Maryland. However, Lee ensured that he was reinstated for the coming fight, and it was the arrival of Hill's division at Antietam that saved the day for the Confederates. He was slightly wounded by friendly fire at Chancellorsville and was given command of the newly created Third Corps before Gettysburg. Hill, a fine division commander, could not seem to adapt to the new position, although his declining health might have been partly to blame. In October, he launched an unfortunate attack at Bristoe Station and suffered significant casualties. He fought at the Wilderness, but owing to his declining health, he had to relinquish his command at Spotsylvania. Hill returned at Cold Harbor and did solid work, leading his diminished corps in the Petersburg Campaign. As Grant launched his final assault at Petersburg on April 2, 1865, Hill was shot and killed. He is buried under his statue on Laburnum Avenue in Richmond, Virginia.[185]

Theophilus Hunter Holmes

Unsatisfied with Holmes's performance during the Peninsula Campaign, Lee had him transferred to the Trans-Mississippi Department. According to accounts, he was disagreeable and would "cuss and roar" and "bawl out" his staff. Despite this, he was promoted to lieutenant general in October 1862. He seemed focused on only his area, not helping others in need, and did not add anything of value to his assignment. In March 1863, he was relieved of command and sent to Arkansas. By early 1864, Kirby Smith and the governors of Arkansas and Missouri, as well as the Arkansas Congressional delegation, were petitioning Richmond for his removal. Rather than be discharged, Holmes resigned on March 16. He was then assigned command of the reserves in North Carolina. Following the war, he farmed in North Carolina and died on January 21, 1880. He is buried in Fayetteville.[186]

Benjamin Huger

Huger was another officer whose performance during the campaign led to his reassignment. On August 26, he was appointed inspector of artillery and ordnance for the army, but the head of ordnance, Josiah Gorgas, ignored him. In March 1863, he was sent to the Trans-Mississippi to inspect ordnance and was to report to Kirby Smith. After the war, he lived in Fauquier County, Virginia, before returning to Charleston, South Carolina, where he died on December 7, 1877. He is buried at Green Mount Cemetery in Baltimore.[187]

Thomas Jonathan Jackson

Sent to deal with the other major Federal army in Virginia under John Pope, Jackson scored a victory on August 9 at Cedar Mountain. He next moved around Pope's flank and into the Union rear, setting the stage for the spectacular Confederate victory at Second Manassas. During the invasion of Maryland, he captured some twelve thousand Federal soldiers, as well as artillery and supplies, at Harper's Ferry. Jackson then rushed to Sharpsburg and played a major role in holding off the Federal attacks. He was promoted to lieutenant general on October 11 and assigned command of the newly formed Second Corps. In December, he commanded the right wing of the Confederate army at Fredericksburg, and at Chancellorsville, he executed his legendary flank march and crushed the Union right. As darkness fell on that battlefield, he continued to search for opportunities to further damage the enemy; hearing horsemen and unable to see clearly, Jackson's own men shot him. His left arm was amputated, but pneumonia set in. Jackson died on May 10, 1863. He is buried in Lexington, Virginia.[188]

Micah Jenkins

When Lee organized the army into two wings, Jenkins was promoted to brigadier general, effective July 22. In Longstreet's corps, he participated at Second Manassas, where he was severely wounded. He returned to action in November and served in Pickett's division. Jenkins was involved in the Suffolk, Virginia campaign, and when Longstreet departed for the northern invasion, Jenkins and his South Carolinians were left in the Suffolk area. His brigade later accompanied Longstreet to northern Georgia. Jenkins's unit arrived too late to participate in the Battle of Chickamauga, but he assumed command of Hood's division following the latter's wounding. He participated throughout Longstreet's Tennessee Campaign. In March 1864, he resumed command of his South Carolina brigade, and the entire corps returned to the Army of Northern Virginia on May 2. At the Battle of the Wilderness, Jenkins was scouting forward in preparation for an attack but was mortally wounded by friendly fire as he and Longstreet rode through the woods. He died soon after and is buried in Charleston, South Carolina.[189]

Robert E. Lee

After the campaign, Lee continued with a string of victories at Second Manassas, Fredericksburg and Chancellorsville. This victorious run was interrupted only by the standoff at Sharpsburg (Antietam). After defeating Joseph Hooker at Chancellorsville, Lee took his army north, where it was defeated at Gettysburg. Following that crushing blow, Lee's army lost much of its ability to strike hard blows, but it managed to hold off the Union army time and time again with defensive actions. However, the war of attrition was being lost, and eventually his army was hemmed in around Petersburg and Richmond. When U.S. Grant finally stretched the Confederates to the breaking point at Five Forks, Lee was forced to abandon Richmond and Petersburg. His army was cut off at Appomattox, where he surrendered on April 9, 1865. In the years after the war, Lee served as the president of Washington College (later named Washington and Lee), where he could try to develop young men for leadership. He died at the school on October 12, 1870, and is buried there.[190]

James Longstreet

One of the most controversial commanders in the Army of Northern Virginia, Longstreet was also one of Lee's most valued subordinates. He launched a devastating attack at Second Manassas and fought at Sharpsburg (Antietam) and Fredericksburg but missed the action at Chancellorsville, as he was assigned to a campaign in the Suffolk, Virginia area. At Gettysburg, he disagreed with Lee's plan, and his controversial record began. He was sent to Tennessee and fought well at Chickamauga but not as well at Knoxville. Returning to Virginia in 1864, Longstreet was wounded by his own troops at the Wilderness in a manner strangely reminiscent of the way in which Jackson was wounded nearby a year earlier. He returned to the Army of Northern Virginia in October and remained active until Appomattox. Following the war, he became a Republican and endorsed his old friend U.S. Grant. Longstreet was appointed to a number of government posts, including minister to Turkey. These actions did not endear him to die-hard southerners, and he compounded that with his memoirs, which contained criticism of Lee. Despite all of his critics, Longstreet should be remembered as the one Lee trusted the most, especially after the loss of Jackson. He died in Gainesville, Georgia, on January 2, 1904, and is buried there at the Alta Vista Cemetery.[191]

John Bankhead Magruder

After hours of marching and countermarching at Glendale, things would get even worse for Magruder the following day. At Malvern Hill, he seemed to be highly agitated and not under control. Whether this was due to lack of sleep, medication, nerves or a combination of everything, it didn't matter. The inability to control one's composure was not something Lee could tolerate in a leader. When the Seven Days Campaign ended, Magruder was quickly transferred to the Trans-Mississippi area. By October, he was in Texas, guarding its coast. On January 1, 1863, he captured Galveston. Magruder remained in Texas until the war's end and then ventured to Mexico to serve in Emperor Maximilian's army. When the latter fell, Magruder returned to Texas, where he died on February 18, 1871. He is buried in Galveston.[192]

FEDERAL[193]

Samuel P. Heintzelman

At Second Manassas under Pope, Heintzelman led an attack against Jackson that was repulsed. He was later assigned to the command of part of the Washington defenses and to court-martial duty. Following the war, he served in Texas and retired in 1869 as a major general. Heintzelman died in Washington on May 1, 1880, and is buried at Forest Lawn Cemetery in Buffalo, New York.

Joseph Hooker

A solid division leader, Hooker was promoted to army command after Burnside's disastrous Fredericksburg campaign. He led the Union army at

Chancellorsville, where his army was crushed in what may have been Lee's most spectacular victory. Following that battle, Hooker screened Washington and Baltimore against the Confederates' northern invasion, and when he requested that reinforcements be sent to him from Harper's Ferry, he was refused. Hooker offered his resignation from command of the Army of the Potomac, which was accepted. He was moved to the Western Theater, and at Chattanooga, he drove the Confederates from Lookout Mountain. Hooker remained in active service until his retirement in 1868. He died in Garden City, New York, on October 31, 1879, and is buried in Cincinnati.

George A. McCall

At Glendale, McCall rode into the 47th Virginia and was captured. He was released from Libby Prison in August 1862, exchanged for Confederate general Simon Bolivar Buckner. McCall remained on sick leave until he was reassigned in March 1863. He died on February 2, 1868, and is buried at Christ Church Cemetery in Philadelphia.

Philip Kearny

Kearny was promoted to major general on July 4. Following the battle at Second Manassas, he inadvertently rode into the Confederate lines at Ox Hill and was killed—a great loss to the Federal cause. He created the "Kearny Patch," the precursor to Federal corps patches. Originally buried at Trinity Church Cemetery in New York City, his remains were later moved to Arlington.

George B. McClellan

Following the Seven Days, McClellan's army was sent north, and as his units arrived in Alexandria, they were transferred to the command of John Pope. After Pope's disastrous performance at Second Manassas, McClellan was again assigned command of the army in an effort to reorganize it and to restore morale. Both of these were his strong points. He fought Lee to a draw at Sharpsburg, where the latter was undermanned and in a very precarious situation. McClellan did not promptly follow Lee into Virginia and was relieved on November 11. In 1864, McClellan was nominated for president by the Democratic Party but was defeated by Lincoln. He served as governor of New Jersey from 1878 to 1881. McClellan died on October 29, 1885, and is buried at Riverview Cemetery in Trenton, New Jersey.

Israel B. Richardson

Richardson was a descendant of Revolutionary War general Israel Putnam. On July 5, 1862, he was promoted to major general, and in September, he fought savagely at the "Bloody Lane" at Sharpsburg. While directing a field battery there, Richardson was hit by a piece of shrapnel and was taken to the Pry house, where he died on November 3. He is buried in Pontiac, Michigan.

John Sedgwick

Wounded at Glendale, Sedgwick was promoted to major general on July 25. At Sharpsburg, he was wounded three more times. He commanded the left wing of Hooker's army at Chancellorsville and led the attacks against Marye's Heights. Sedgwick's Sixth Corps was held in reserve at Gettysburg. He fought at Rappahannock Bridge in November 1863 and at the Wilderness the following May. Sedgwick was killed by a sharpshooter at Spotsylvania on May 9, 1864. He is buried in Cornwall Hollow, Connecticut.

Henry W. Slocum

Promoted to major general on July 25, Slocum helped to cover Pope's retreat from Second Manassas. He fought in the Maryland Campaign but not at Fredericksburg. Slocum commanded a corps at Chancellorsville and Gettysburg. He was transferred to Chattanooga and then to Vicksburg. Slocum was assigned to the command of the Twentieth Corps and led it into Atlanta. He commanded Sherman's left on the "March to the Sea." Slocum resigned from the army on September 25, 1865, and later served three terms in Congress, as well as served on the Gettysburg Monument Commission. He died in Brooklyn, New York, on April 14, 1894, and is buried at Green-Wood Cemetery.

Edwin V. Sumner

Sumner was born in 1797, the oldest of the Union field commanders, and was known as "Bull Head." He was promoted to major general on July 16, 1862. He fought at Sharpsburg and commanded the "Left Grand Division" at Fredericksburg. Sumner asked to be relieved when Hooker was assigned command of the army and was assigned to the Department of Missouri. He died on March 21, 1863, and is buried at Oakwood Cemetery in Syracuse, New York.

George Sykes

Sykes commanded the Union "Regulars" and fought at Second Manassas but was held in reserve at Sharpsburg and Fredericksburg. He was promoted to major general on November 29, 1862. Sykes was at Chancellorsville but was not involved in Hooker's rout. He held the Federal left at Gettysburg and participated in the Mine Run Campaign, but army commander George Meade was not satisfied with his performance; Slocum was relieved in December 1863. He was sent to Kansas in the spring of 1864. He died in Brownsville, Texas, in February 1880 and is buried at West Point.

Order of Battle

Union: Army of the Potomac
Maj. Gen. George B. McClellan[194]

Second Corps
Brig. Gen. Edwin V. Sumner

First Division
Brig. Gen. Israel B. Richardson

First Brigade
Brig. Gen. John C. Caldwell
5th New Hampshire
7th New York
61st New York
Massachusetts Sharpshooters Co. 1
81st Pennsylvania

Second Brigade
Brig. Gen. T.F. Meagher
29th Massachusetts
63rd New York
69th New York
88th New York

Second Division
Brig. Gen. John Sedgwick

First Brigade
Col. Alfred Sully
15th Massachusetts
1st Minnesota
34th New York
82nd New York
Russell's Company Sharpshooters

Second Brigade
Brig. Gen. William W. Burns
69th Pennsylvania
71st Pennsylvania
72nd Pennsylvania
106th Pennsylvania

Third Brigade
Brig. Gen. William H. French
52nd New York
57th New York
64th New York
66th New York
53rd Pennsylvania
2nd Delaware

Third Brigade
Brig. Gen. N.J.T. Dana
19th Massachusetts
20th Massachusetts
7th Michigan
42nd New York

Artillery
Capt. George W. Hazzard
1st New York Light, Battery B
4th U.S., Batteries A and C

Artillery
Col. Charles H. Tompkins
1st Rhode Island Light, Battery A
1st U.S., Battery I

Corps Artillery Reserve
1st New York Light, Battery G
1st Rhode Island Light, Batteries B and G

Cavalry
6th New York Cavalry, companies D, F, H, and K

Third Corps
Brig. Gen. Samuel P. Heintzelman

Second Division
Brig. Gen. Joseph Hooker

First Brigade
Brig. Gen. Cuvier Grover
1st Massachusetts
11th Massachusetts
16th Massachusetts
2nd New Hampshire
26th Pennsylvania

Second Brigade
Brig. Gen. Daniel E. Sickles
70th New York
71st New York
72nd New York
73rd New York
74th New York

Third Division
Brig. Gen. Philip Kearny

First Brigade
Brig. Gen. John C. Robinson
20th Indiana
87th New York
57th Pennsylvania
63rd Pennsylvania
105th Pennsylvania

Second Brigade
Brig. Gen. David B. Birney
3rd Maine
4th Maine
38th New York
40th New York
101st New York

Third Brigade
Col. Joseph B. Carr
5th New Jersey
6th New Jersey
7th New Jersey
8th New Jersey
2nd New York

Artillery
1st New York Light, Battery D
New York Light, 4th Battery
1st U.S. Light, Battery H

Corps Artillery Reserve
Capt. Gustavus A. De Russy
New York Light, 6th Battery
New Jersey Light, 2nd Battery
4th U.S., Battery K

Cavalry
Col. William W. Averell
3rd Pennsylvania

Third Brigade
Brig. Gen. Hiram G. Berry
2nd Michigan
3rd Michigan
5th Michigan
1st New York
37th New York

1st Rhode Island Light, Battery E
2nd U.S., Battery G

Fourth Corps
Brig. Gen. Erasmus D. Keyes

First Division
Brig. Gen. Darius N Couch

First Brigade
Brig. Gen. Albion P. Howe
55th New York
62nd New York
93rd Pennsylvania
98th Pennsylvania
102nd Pennsylvania

Second Brigade
Brig. Gen. John J. Abercrombie
65th New York
67th New York

Second Division
Brig. Gen. John J. Peck

First Brigade
Brig. Gen. Henry N. Naglee
11th Maine
56th New York
100th New York
52nd Pennsylvania
104th Pennsylvania

Second Brigade
Brig. Gen. Henry W. Wessels
81st New York
85th New York

23rd Pennsylvania
31st Pennsylvania
61st Pennsylvania

Third Brigade
Brig. Gen. Innis N. Palmer
7th Massachusetts
10th Massachusetts
36th New York
2nd Rhode Island

Artillery
1st Pennsylvania Light, Batteries C, D
New York Light, 7th Battery

92nd New York
96th New York
98th New York
85th Pennsylvania
101st Pennsylvania
103rd Pennsylvania

Artillery
1st New York Light, Battery H

Corps Reserve Artillery
Maj. Robert M. West
New York Light, 8th Battery
1st Pennsylvania Light, Batteries E, H
5th U.S. Artillery, Battery M

Cavalry
Col. D. McM. Gregg
8th Pennsylvania Cavalry

Ffith Corps
Brig. Gen. Fitz John Porter

First Division
Brig. Gen. George W. Morell

First Brigade
Brig. Gen. John H. Martindale
2nd Maine
18th Massachusetts
22nd Massachusetts
1st Michigan
13th New York
25th New York
Massachusetts Sharpshooters (2nd Co.)

Second Division
Brig. Gen. George Sykes

First Brigade
Col. Robert C. Buchanan
3rd U.S. Infantry
4th U.S, Infantry
12th U.S. Infantry
14th U.S. Infantry

Second Brigade
Brig. Gen. Charles Griffin
9th Massachusetts
4th Michigan
14th New York
62nd Pennsylvania

Second Brigade
Maj. Charles S. Lovell
2nd U.S. Infantry
6th U.S. Infantry
10th U.S. Infantry
11th U.S. Infantry
17th U.S. Infantry

Third Brigade
Brig. Gen. Daniel Butterfield
12th New York
17th New York
44th New York
16th Michigan
Brady's Company, Michigan Sharpshooters
83rd Pennsylvania

Third Brigade
Col. G.K. Warren
5th New York
10th New York

Artillery
Capt. William B. Weeden
Massachusetts Light, 3rd Battery C
Massachusetts Light, 5th Battery E
1st Rhode Island Light, Battery C
5th U.S. Artillery, Battery D

Artillery
Capt. Stephen H. Weed
3rd U.S., Batteries L, M
5th U.S., Battery I

Sharpshooters
Col. Hiram Berdan
1st U.S. Sharpshooters

Third Division
Brig. Gen. George A. McCall

First Brigade
Col. Seneca G. Simmons
(Brig. Gen. Reynolds captured)
1st Pennsylvania Reserves
2nd Pennsylvania Reserves
5th Pennsylvania Reserves
8th Pennsylvania Reserves
13th Pennsylvania Reserves (1st Rifles)

Second Brigade
Brig. Gen. George G. Meade
3rd Pennsylvania Reserves
4th Pennsylvania Reserves
7th Pennsylvania Reserves
11th Pennsylvania Reserves

Third Brigade
Brig. Gen. Truman Seymour
6th Pennsylvania Reserves
9th Pennsylvania Reserves
10th Pennsylvania Reserves
12th Pennsylvania Reserves

Artillery
1st Pennsylvania Light Artillery. Batteries A, B, G
5th U.S. Artillery, Battery C

Cavalry
4th Pennsylvania Cavalry
8th Illinois Cavalry

Artillery Reserve
Col. Henry J. Hunt

First Brigade (Horse Artillery)
Lt. Col. William Hays
2nd U.S., Batteries A, B, L, M
3rd U.S., Batteries C and G

Third Brigade
Maj. Albert Arndt
1st Battalion New York Light
Batteries A, B, C, D

Fifth Brigade
Capt. J. Howard Carlisle
2nd U.S., Battery E
3rd U.S., Batteries F and K

Unattached
1st New York, Battery G
New York Light, 5th Battery

Siege Train
Col. Robert O. Tyler
1st Connecticut Heavy Artillery

Second Brigade
Lt. Col. George W. Getty
1st U.S., Batteries E, G, K
4th U.S., Battery G
5th U.S., Batteries A, K

Fourth Brigade
Maj. E.R. Petherbridge
Maryland Light, Batteries A, B

Sixth Corps
Brig. Gen. William B. Franklin

FIRST DIVISION
Brig. Gen. Henry W. Slocum

First Brigade
Brig. Gen. George W. Taylor
1st New Jersey
2nd New Jersey
3rd New Jersey
4th New Jersey

Second Brigade
Col. Joseph J. Bartlett
5th Maine
16th New York
27th New York
966h Pennsylvania

Third Brigade
Brig. Gen. John Newton
18th New York
31st New York
32nd New York
95th Pennsylvania

Artillery
Capt. Edward R. Platt
Massachusetts Light, Battery A
New Jersey Light, 1st Battery
2nd U.S. Artillery, Battery D

SECOND DIVISION
Brig. Gen. William F. Smith

First Brigade
Brig. Gen. W.S. Hancock
6th Maine
43rd New York
49th Pennsylvania
5th Wisconsin

Second Brigade
Brig. Gen. W.T.H. Brooks
2nd Vermont
3rd Vermont
4th Vermont
5th Vermont
6th Vermont

Third Brigade
Brig. Gen. John W. Davidson
7th Maine
20th New York
33rd New York
49th New York
77th New York

Artillery
Capt. Romeyn B. Ayers
1st New York Light, Battery E
New York Light, 1st Battery
New York Light, 3rd Battery
5th U.S., Battery F

Cavalry
5th Pennsylvania, Companies J, K

Unattached Cavalry
1st New York

Cavalry Reserve
Brig. Gen. Philip St. George Cooke
6th Pennsylvania
1st U.S., Companies A, C, F, H
5th U.S. Cavalry, Companies A, D, F, H, I
6th U.S. Cavalry

Volunteer Engineers Brigade
Brig. Gen. Daniel P. Woodbury
15th New York Engineers
50th New York Engineers

***

CONFEDERATE: ARMY OF NORTHERN VIRGINIA GEN. ROBERT E. LEE[195]

Jackson's Command

WHITING'S DIVISION
Brig. Gen. William H.C. Whiting

Hood's Texas Brigade
Brig. Gen. John B. Hood
18th Georgia
1st Texas
4th Texas
5th Texas
Hampton Legion (South Carolina)

Allegheny (Virginia) Battery

Rockbridge (Virginia) Battery

Law's Brigade
Col. Evander M. Law
4th Alabama
2nd Mississippi
11th Mississippi
6th North Carolina
Richmond Hampden (Virginia) Battery

JACKSON'S DIVISION

Winder's Brigade
Brig. Gen. Charles S. Winder
2nd Virginia
4th Virginia
5th Virginia
27th Virginia
33rd Virginia

Jones' Brigade
Brig. Gen. John R. Jones
21st Virginia
42nd Virginia
48th Virginia
1st Virginia Battalion (Irish)

Artillery
Staunton (Virginia) Battery
Rowan (North Carolina) Battery

Unattached Artillery
Jackson (Virginia) Battery

EWELL'S DIVISION
Maj. Gen. Richard S. Ewell

Elzey's Brigade
Brig. Gen. Jubal A. Early
12th Georgia
13th Virginia
25th Virginia
31st Virginia
44th Virginia
52nd Virginia
58th Virginia

Trimble's Brigade
Brig. Gen. I.R. Trimble
15th Alabama
21st Georgia
16th Mississippi
21st North Carolina
1st North Carolina Battalion
Henrico (Virginia) Battery

Fulkerson's Brigade
Brig. Gen. Wade Hampton
10th Virginia
23rd Virginia
37th Virginia
Danville (Virginia) Battery

Lawton's Brigade
Brig. Gen. A.E. Lawton
13th Georgia
26th Georgia
31st Georgia
38th Georgia
60th Georgia (4th Battalion)
61st Georgia

D.H. HILL'S DIVISION
Maj. Gen. Daniel H. Hill

Rodes' Brigade
Brig. Gen. Robert E. Rodes
3rd Alabama
5th Alabama
6th Alabama
12th Alabama
26th Alabama

G.B. Anderson's Brigade
Brig. Gen. George B. Anderson
2nd North Carolina
4th North Carolina
14th North Carolina
30th North Carolina

Taylor's Brigade
Brig. Gen. Richard Taylor
6th Louisiana
7th Louisiana
8th Louisiana
9th Louisiana
1st Louisiana Special Battalion
Charlottesville (Virginia) Battery

Maryland Line
Col. Bradley T. Johnson
First Maryland
Baltimore (Maryland) Battery

Garland's Brigade
Brig. Gen. Samuel Garland
5th North Carolina
12th North Carolina
13th North Carolina
20th North Carolina
23rd North Carolina

Colquitt's Brigade
Col. A.H. Colquitt
13th Alabama
6th Georgia
23rd Georgia
27th Georgia
28th Georgia

Ripley's Brigade
Brig. Gen. Roswell. S. Ripley
44th Georgia
48th Georgia
1st North Carolina
3rd North Carolina

Artillery
Jeff. Davis Battery (Alabama) Battery
King William (Virginia) Battery
Long Island (Virginia) Battery (temporarily attached)
Hardaway's (Alabama) Battery
Hanover (Virginia) Battery
Richmond Orange (Virginia) Battery (temporarily attached)
Rhett's (South Carolina) Battery (temporarily attached)

Magruder's Command

Jones' Division
Brig. Gen. David R. Jones

Toombs' Brigade
Brig. Gen. Robert Toombs
2nd Georgia
15th Georgia
17th Georgia

McLaws' Division
Maj. Gen. Lafayette McLaws

Semmes' Brigade
Brig. Gen. Paul J. Semmes
10th Georgia
53rd Georgia
5th Louisiana

20th Georgia

10th Louisiana
15th Virginia
32nd Virginia
Manly's (North Carolina) Battery

G.T. Anderson's Brigade
Col. George T. Anderson
1st Georgia (Regulars)
7th Georgia
8th Georgia
9th Georgia
11th Georgia

Kershaw's Brigade
Brig. Gen. J.B. Kershaw
2nd South Carolina
3rd South Carolina
7th South Carolina
8th South Carolina
Alexandria (Virginia) Battery

Artillery
Wise (Virginia) Battery
Washington (South Carolina) Battery
Sumter (Georgia) Battery, Co. E (temporarily attached)
Madison (Louisiana) Battery
Ashland (Virginia) Battery (temporarily attached)
Dabney's (Virginia) Battery

MAGRUDER'S DIVISION
Cobb's Brigade
Brig. Gen. Howell Cobb
16th Georgia
24th Georgia
Cobb's (Georgia) Legion
2nd Louisiana
15th North Carolina

Troup (Georgia) Battery

Griffith's Brigade
Brig. Gen. R. Griffith
13th Mississippi
17th Mississippi
18th Mississippi
21st Mississippi
1st Co. Richmond Howitzers (Virginia)

Artillery
Col. S.D. Lee
Amherst (Virginia) Battery
Magruder (Virginia) Battery
Pulaski (Virginia) Battery
James City (Virginia) Battery

LONGSTREET'S DIVISION*
Maj. Gen. James Longstreet

Kemper's Brigade
Brig. Gen. James L. Kemper
1st Virginia
7th Virginia
11th Virginia
17th Virginia
24th Virginia
Loudoun (Virginia) Battery

R.H. *Anderson's Brigade*
Brig. Gen. R.H. Anderson
Col. Micah Jenkins
2nd South Carolina Rifles
4th South Carolina
5th South Carolina
6th South Carolina
Palmetto (South Carolina) Sharpshooters

Pickett's Brigade
Brig. Gen. George E. Pickett
Col. Eppa Hunton
Col. J.B. Strange
8th Virginia
18th Virginia
19th Virginia
28th Virginia
56th Virginia

Wilcox's Brigade
Brig. Gen. Cadmus Wilcox
8th Alabama
9th Alabama
10th Alabama
11th Alabama
Thomas (Virginia) Battery

Pryor's Brigade
Brig. Gen. Roger A. Pryor
14th Alabama
2nd Florida
14th Louisiana
1st Louisiana Battalion
3rd Virginia
Donaldsonville (Louisiana) Battery

Featherston's Brigade
Brig. Gen. W.S. Featherston
12th Mississippi
19th Mississippi
2nd Mississippi Battalion
3rd Richmond Howitzers, Co. 3

Artillery
Washington Artillery Battalion (Louisiana), Companies 1, 2, 3, 4
Lynchburg (Virginia) Battery
Dixie (Virginia) Battery

**Note:* Longstreet's command was divided into demi-divisions, with Wilcox leading three brigades and R.H. Anderson the other three.

HUGER'S DIVISION
Maj. Gen. Benjamin Huger

Mahone's Brigade
Brig. Gen. William Mahone

Wright's Brigade
Brig. Gen. A.R. Wright

6th Virginia
12th Virginia
16th Virginia
41st Virginia
49th Virginia
Portsmouth (Virginia) Battery
Lynchburg Beauregard (Virginia) Battery

44th Alabama
3rd Georgia
4th Georgia
22nd Georgia
1st Louisiana
Virginia Light Artillery, Co. D
Sumter (Georgia) Artillery, Co. A

Armistead's Brigade
Brig. Gen. Lewis Armistead
9th Virginia
14th Virginia
38th Virginia
53rd Virginia
57th Virginia
5th Virginia Battalion
Fauquier (Virginia) Battery
Goochland (Virginia) Battery

HILL'S LIGHT DIVISION
Maj. Gen. Ambrose P. Hill

Field's Brigade
Brig. Gen. Charles W. Field
40th Virginia
47th Virginia
55th Virginia
60th Virginia

Gregg's Brigade
Brig. Gen. Maxcy Gregg
1st South Carolina
1st South Carolina Rifles
12th South Carolina
13th South Carolina
14th South Carolina

J.R. Anderson's Brigade
Brig. Gen. Joseph R. Anderson
14th Georgia
35th Georgia
45th Georgia
49th Georgia
3rd Louisiana Battalion

Branch's Brigade
Brig. Gen. L. O'Bryan Branch
7th North Carolina
18th North Carolina
28th North Carolina
33rd North Carolina
37th North Carolina

Archer's Brigade
Brig. Gen. James J. Archer
5th Alabama Battalion

Pender's Brigade
Brig. Gen. William D. Pender
2nd Arkansas Battalion

19th Georgia
1st Tennessee
7th Tennessee
14th Tennessee
16th North Carolina
22nd North Carolina
34th North Carolina
38th North Carolina
22nd Virginia Battalion

Artillery
Lt. Col. Lewis M. Coleman
1st Maryland Battcry
Charleston (South Carolina) German Battery
Fredericksburg (Virginia) Battery
Crenshaw's (Virginia) Battery
Letcher's (Virginia) Battery
Johnson's (Virginia) Battery
Masters' (Virginia) Battery
Pee Dee (South Carolina) Battery
Purcell (Virginia) Battery

Holmes' Division
Maj. Gen. Theophilus H. Holmes

Ransom's Brigade
Brig. Gen. Robert Ransom Jr.
24th North Carolina
25th North Carolina
26th North Carolina
35th North Carolina
48th North Carolina
49th North Carolina

Daniel's Brigade
Brig. Gen. Junius Daniel
43rd North Carolina
45th North Carolina
50th North Carolina
Burroughs' Battalion (Cavalry)

Walker's Brigade
Brig. Gen. J.G. Walker
3rd Arkansas
2nd Georgia Battalion
27th North Carolina
46th North Carolina
30th Virginia
Goodwyn's Cavalry

Artillery
Branch's (Virginia) Battery
Brem's (North Carolina) Battery
French's (Virginia) Battery
Graham's (Virginia) Battery
Grandy's (Virginia) Battery
Lloyd's (North Carolina) Battery

Wise's Command
Brig. Gen. Henry A. Wise

26th Virginia
46th Virginia

4th Virginia Heavy Artillery
10th Virginia Cavalry
Andrews' (Alabama) Battery
Armistead's (Virginia) Battery
French's (Virginia) Battery
Nelson (Virginia) Battery

Reserve Artillery
Brig. Gen. W.N. Pendleton

1st Virginia Artillery
Col. J. Thompson Brown
Williamsburg (Virginia) Artillery
Richmond Fayette Battery
2nd Co. Richmond Howitzers

Jones' Battalion
Maj. H.P. Jones
Long Island (Virginia) Battery
Orange Richmond (Virginia) Battery
Rhett's (South Carolina) Battery

Richardson's Battalion
Maj. Charles Richardson
Fluvanna (Virginia) Battery
Milledge's (Georgia) Battery
Ashland (Virginia) Battery

Sumter's (Georgia) Battalion
Lieut. Col. A.S. Cutts
Blackshear's Company
Lane's Company
Price's Company
Ross' Company
Hamilton's Battery

Nelson's Battalion
Maj. William Nelson
Fluvanna (Virginia) Battery
Amherst (Virginia) Battery
Morris (Virginia) Battery

Cavalry
Brig. Gen. James E.B. Stuart
1st North Carolina
1st Virginia
3rd Virginia
4th Virginia
5th Virginia
9th Virginia
10th Virginia
Cobb's (Georgia) Legion
Critcher's (Virginia) Battalion

Hampton's (South Carolina) Legion
Jeff. Davis Legion
Stuart Horse Artillery
Chew's (Virginia) Battery

Notes

Abbreviations for cited sources:

OR: U.S. War Department, *War of the Rebellion.* All citations are to series 1, volume 11, part 2 unless otherwise noted.

LOC: Library of Congress.

RNBP: Richmond National Battlefield Park.

Chapter 1

1. Burton, *Extraordinary Circumstances*, 13.
2. Hartwig, *To Antietam Creek*, 62–63.
3. *OR*, 490, Lee's report of March 6, 1863.
4. Ibid., 553, Jackson's report, February 20, 1863.
5. Ibid., 38–41, Union casualty returns; Sears, *To the Gates of Richmond*, 249; Burton, *Extraordinary Circumstances*, 136.

Chapter 2

6. Hartwig, *To Antietam Creek*, 142–44.
7. Ibid., 83–86, 158–60; Alexander, *Fighting for the Confederacy*, 62.

Chapter 3

8. *OR*, 493–94, Lee's report of March 6, 1863; Burton, *Extraordinary Circumstances*, 156.
9. For McClellan, two other roads existed slightly to the east, one at Smith's Store and one past Samaria Church; these were roughly three and five miles away and were used by the Army of the Potomac in 1864. Williams, *Lincoln*

finds a General, 233–34; Sears, *To the Gates of Richmond*, 256–57. Sears adds that another, closer road was discovered and later used "by accident."

10. The sleepy crossroads was also known by other names, such as "New Market," "Frayser's Farm," "Charles City Crossroads," "Riddell's Shop" and "Nelson's Farm." The battle would come to be known by all of these.
11. *OR*, 192–95, Keyes's report of July 20, 1862; 525, Baker's report of July 27, 1862; 532–33, Rosser's report of July 26, 1862; 235, Averell's report of July 7, 1862; Rhodes, *All for the Union*, 64; Manarin, *Henrico County Field of Honor*, 157–59.
12. *OR*, 494, Lee's report of March 6, 1863.
13. *OR*, 662, Magruder's report of August 12, 1862; Sears, *To the Gates of Richmond*, 263–64; letter of Edward E. Davis, 1st Minnesota, July 5, 1862, Davis Papers, photocopy at RNBP, bound volume no. 199; Rafuse, *McClellan's War*, 226; Rhodes, *All for the Union*, 64.
14. *OR*, 21–22, McClellan's report of July 15, 1862; Rafuse, *McClellan's War*, 226; Sears, *To the Gates of Richmond*, 267; Williams, *Lincoln Finds a General*, 235.
15. *OR*, 662–64, Magruder's report of August 12, 1862; 675, D.R. Jones letter to Magruder, June 28, 1862; vol. 11, part 3, 625, D.R. Jones letter to Magruder, June 29, 1862. This was the same letter, sent on two different days. Both notes are cited as a point of interest.
16. Sears, *To the Gates of Richmond*, 265–66.
17. Franklin, "Rear-Guard Fighting," 371–73.
18. *OR*, 494, Lee's report of March 6, 1862; 664, Magruder's report of August 12, 1862; Sears, *To the Gates of Richmond*, 266–67; Manarin, *Henrico County Field of Honor*, 166–67.
19. Freeman, *R.E. Lee*, 174.
20. *OR*, 716, McLaws's report of July 20, 1862; 726, Kershaw's report of July 17, 1862.
21. Franklin, "Rear-Guard Fighting," 372–73.
22. *OR*, 726–27, Kershaw's report; 735, James D. Nance's report of July 11, 1862; 741, Aiken's report of July 10, 1862; 747, Stephen D. Lee's report of July 22, 1862.
23. Ibid., 91–92, Burns's report; Burton, *Extraordinary Circumstances*, 215.
24. *OR*, 720–21, Semmes's report of July 4, 1862.
25. Ibid., 476–77, Brooks's report, of July 19, 1862; 479, Grant's report of July 9, 1862.
26. Ibid., 740–41, Aiken's report of July 10, 1862; 743, Henegan's report of July 14, 1862; Burton, *Extraordinary Circumstances*, 219–20.
27. *OR*, 750, Barksdale's report of July 24, 1862.
28. Ibid., 99, Heintzelman's report of July 21, 1862.
29. Dowdey and Manarin, *Wartime Papers of Robert E. Lee*, 205.
30. *OR*, 665, Magruder's report of August 12, 1862; Sears, *To the Gates of Richmond*, 274; Burton, *Extraordinary Circumstances*, 221–23.
31. Burton, *Extraordinary Circumstances*, 221; Manarin, *Henrico County Field of Honor*, 188.
32. *Charleston Daily Courier*, July 22, 1862, quoted in Wyckoff, *History of the 3rd South Carolina*.
33. Letter from Robert Boyd to his father, July 6, 1862, photocopy at RNBP, bound volume no. 47.

34. Sears, *To the Gates of Richmond*, 269; letter from M.A. Miller to Jed. Hotchkiss, May 26, 1896, photocopy at RNBP, bound volume no. 19.
35. Alexander, *Military Memoirs of a Confederate*, 136; Alexander, *Fighting for the Confederacy*, 105–6.
36. Robertson, *Stonewall Jackson*, 488–89. Robertson cites a letter for R.H. Chilton to J.E.B. Stuart dated June 29.
37. Hartwig, *To Antietam Creek*, 69.

CHAPTER 4

38. Franklin, "Rear-Guard Fighting," 375.
39. *OR*, 55, Richardson's report of July 6, 1862; George W. Batchelder Papers; Mason, *Until Antietam*, 158.
40. Franklin, "Rear-Guard Fighting," 376.
41. Ibid., 376–77.
42. Manarin, *Henrico County Field of Honor*, 203–4; *OR*, 292–94, Martindale's report of March 27, 1863.
43. *OR*, 228, Porter's report of July 8, 1862.
44. Manarin, *Henrico County Field of Honor*, 201–2; *OR*, 913–14, Junius Daniel's report of July 16, 1862.
45. *OR*, 665, Jackson's report of February 20, 1863; 659–60, Magruder's report of August 12, 1863; Hill, "McClellan's Change of Base," 386; Webb, *Peninsula*, 141; Manarin, *Henrico County Field of Honor*, 204.
46. Manarin, *Henrico County Field of Honor*, 209–10. Manarin cites Henry Robinson Berkeley's *Four Years in the Confederate Artillery*, 20, and John Casler's *Four Years in the Stonewall Brigade*, 94; *OR*, 627, D.H. Hill's report of July 3, 1862; Stiles, *Four Years Under Marse Robert*, 95.
47. Stiles, *Four Years Under Marse Robert*, 98–99. It should be noted that historian James Robertson thinks that Stiles's story is a fabrication. He bases this on the fact that it had rained the night before—the ground would have been muddy. Jackson's dust-tinged clothing would have been wet. *Stonewall Jackson*, note 27, page 877. Freeman also doubts its veracity in *Lee's Lieutenants*, vol. 1, 570. Other authors have accepted Stiles's story. The truth cannot be known. Freeman commented, "The essential facts of a conference, at which Jackson appeared alert and aggressive, do not seem open to question."
48. *OR*, 666, Magruder's report of August 12, 1862.

CHAPTER 5

49. Warner, *Generals in Gray*, 143–44.
50. *OR*, 789, Huger's report of July 21, 1862; 494, Lee's report of March 6, 1863.
51. Sears, *To the Gates of Richmond*, 278–79.
52. *OR*, 789, Huger's report of July 21, 1862; 161–62, Kearny's report of July 6, 1862.

53. Ibid., 809, A.R. Wright's report of July 12, 1862; 797, Mahone's report of July 10, 1862; 790, Huger's report of July 21, 1862.
54. Ibid., 798, Mahone's report of July 10, 1862; 435, Slocum's report of July 10, 1862; Burton, *Extraordinary Circumstances*, 24; Manarin, *Henrico County Field of Honor*, 221.
55. Alexander, *Military Memoirs of a Confederate*, 143.
56. *OR*, 906–7, Holmes's report of July 15, 1862; Sears, *To the Gates of Richmond*, 25; Warner, *Generals in Gray*, 141.
57. *OR*, 532, Colonel Thomas Rosser report of July 26, 1862, 532.
58. Ibid., 350, Sykes's report of July 7, 1862; 228, Porter's report of July 8, 1862; 906, Holmes's report of July 15, 1862; Alexander, *Fighting for the Confederacy*, 106; Sears, *To the Gates of Richmond*, 291; Burton, *Extraordinary Circumstances*, 268.
59. *OR*, 907, Holmes's report of July 15, 1862; 228, Porter's report of July 8, 1862; 910, Deshler's report of July 15, 1862.
60. Ibid., 910, Deshler's report of July 15, 1862; 907, Holmes's report of July 15, 1862; Alexander, *Memoirs*, 141; Sears, *To the Gates of Richmond*, 292.
61. *OR*, 911, Deshler's report of July 15, 1862; Hill, "McClellan's Change of Base," 390. Deshler was to be killed later in the war at Missionary Ridge.
62. *OR*, 907–8, Holmes's report of July 15, 1862; 228–29, Porter's report of July 8, 1862.
63. Ibid., 666–67, Magruder's report of August 12, 1862; 675, "Enclosure No. 3," Longstreet's message to Magruder; Freeman, *Lee's Lieutenants*, vol. 1, 584–85; Alexander, *Fighting for the Confederacy*, 107; Sears, *To the Gates of Richmond*, 291.

Chapter 6

64. Dabney, *Life and Campaigns*, 464; Franklin, "Rear-Guard Fighting," 377–78.
65. Franklin, "Rear-Guard Fighting," 378–79; Vandiver, *Mighty Stonewall*, 314; Burton, *Extraordinary Circumstances*, 251; *OR*, 465–66, Ayers's report of July 10, 1862; 561, Crutchfield's report of January 23, 1863. The number of guns is uncertain—Crutchfield said it was twenty-three, Hill said twenty-six, Jackson twenty-eight. The author has opted to go with the artillery commander; 477, Brooks's report of July 9, 1862; 557, Jackson's report of February 20, 1863; 627, D.H. Hill's report (undated); Hill, *Battles & Leaders*, 387; Comte de Paris, *History of the Civil War in America*, 125; Mason, *Until Antietam*, 160; Burton, *Extraordinary Circumstances*, 256; Manarin, *Henrico County Field of Honor*, 212–19; Haskew, *Appomattox*, 157. Most of the Confederate guns were six-pound smoothbores or twelve-pound Napoleons, but there were a few rifled guns. Manarin states that there was one James rifle and two ten-pound Parrotts, as well as two three-inch Burton and Archer guns. The rifled guns had superior range and could fire at the Union guns at the top of the opposing ridge.
66. *OR*, 59, Rufus King's report of July 6, 1862; 561, Crutchfield's report of January 23, 1863; 465–66, Ayers's report of July 10, 1862; 56–57, Pettit's report of July 5, 1862; 655, Rhett's report of July 12, 1862. Rhett discusses the advantage the Federal artillery held with its rifled guns. The Confederacy at this time was disadvantaged in terms of the range of its artillery and the weight of its

ordnance. This shortcoming would be further felt the next day at Malvern Hill and at Antietam (Sharpsburg) in September. It would not be remedied until the following spring; Freeman, *R.E. Lee*, 196; Burton, *Extraordinary Circumstances*, 253.
67. Smith, *Autobiography of Major General William F. Smith*, 46.
68. Franklin, "Rear-Guard Fighting," 379.
69. *OR*, 81, Sedgwick's report of July 5, 1862.
70. Munford letter to John C. Ropes, December 7, 1897, Munford/Ellis papers, Duke University, cited in Robertson, *Stonewall Jackson*, note 37, page 878; Hill, *Battles & Leaders*, 387–88. The comment verifying the story of the Irish soldier was by the editor, who cited *The Century* magazine; Gwynne, *Rebel Yell*, 323.
71. Alexander, *Military Memoirs of a Confederate*, letters from Thomas Munford and Wade Hampton, 149–51; Freeman, *R.E. Lee*, 197.
72. *OR*, 809–11, report of Ambrose Wright, July 12, 1862; Franklin, "Rear-Guard Fighting," 378–81; Freeman, *R.E. Lee*, 196–97. Freeman noted that other than sending Wright back, Jackson did not seem to make any other effort to communicate with the Confederate leaders south of the swamp.
73. Robertson, *Stonewall Jackson*, note 45, letter from Dabney to Hotchkiss, April 22, 1896, 878; Burton, *Extraordinary Circumstances*, 259.
74. Hill, *Battles & Leaders*, vol. 2, 389.
75. McGuire, "General T.J. ('Stonewall') Jackson," 98.
76. Douglas, *I Rode with Stonewall*, 107; Alexander, *Military Memoirs of a Confederate*, 152–53.
77. Munford letter of December 7, 1897, John C. Ropes Collection, Boston University, photocopy at RNBP, bound volume no. 177.
78. *OR*, 557, Jackson's report of February 20, 1863; Wise, *Long Arm of Lee*, 220.
79. Krick, "Sleepless in the Saddle," 82–85; Gwynne, *Rebel Yell*, 317. Gwynne cites a letter from Pendleton to his mother, June 7, 1862, from W.G. Bean's *Stonewall's Man: Sandie Pendleton*, 364; Thomas Carter quoted by R. Willis in a letter to John Ropes, January 7, 1895, John C. Ropes Collection, Boston University.
80. Krick, "Sleepless in the Saddle," 82.
81. Vandiver, *Mighty Stonewall*, 317.
82. Burton, *Extraordinary Circumstances*, 262, Robertson, *Stonewall Jackson*, 497–98; Sears, *To the Gates of Richmond*, 288; Gwynne, *Rebel Yell*, 377–78.

Chapter 7

83. Powell, *Fifth Army Corps*, 136; Burton, *Extraordinary Circumstances*, 238.
84. The author had never heard the battle referred to as "Turkey Creek" but found that reference in *OR*, 428, Taggart's report of July 4, 1862.
85. Manarin, *Henrico County Field of Honor*, 225–26; Robert Dunkerly, "The Battle of Glendale and the Gravel Hill Community," from *Hallowed Ground*, 2012.
86. *OR*, 254–55, Randol's report of July 7, 1862; 389–90, McCall's report of August 12, 1862; 402–3, Seymour's report of July 15, 1862; Powell, *Fifth Army Corps*, 137; Burton, *Extraordinary Circumstances*, 275–76; Ent, *Pennsylvania Reserves*, 86; Manarin, *Henrico County Field of Honor*, 228–29.

87. *OR*, 390, McCall's report of August 12, 1862; 402–3, Seymour's report of July 15, 1862; Powell, *Fifth Army Corps*, 139; Manarin, *Henrico County Field of Honor*, 227–29; Ent, *Pennsylvania Reserves*, 86; Burton, *Extraordinary Circumstances*, 154, 275. Reynolds was captured on the morning after the battle at Gaines's Mill as he was trying to reach the new Federal lines. He had become separated trying to negotiate the swamp and had rested for the night, but by morning, Confederate troops were all around.
88. *OR*, 123, Grover's report of July 12, 1862; 151, Carr's report of July 8, 1862; 138, Sickles's report of July 9, 1862; 111, Hooker's report of July 15, 1862; Manarin, *Henrico County Field of Honor*, 227; Jones, Wilmer, *Generals in Blue and Gray*, vol. 1, 235.
89. *OR*, 111, Hooker's report of July 15, 1862; 151, Carr's report of July 8, 1862; Ent, *Pennsylvania Reserves*, 86, 90.
90. *OR*, 162, Kearny's report of July 6, 1862.
91. Ibid., 838, Hill's report of February 28, 1863.
92. Ibid., 759, Longstreet's report of July 29, 1862; Longstreet, "Seven Days, Including Frayser's Farm," *Battles & Leaders* vol. 2, 400–401.
93. Manarin, *Henrico County Field of Honor*, 232–34; Freeman, *R.E. Lee*, 186.
94. *OR*, 390, McCall's report of August 12, 1862; Powell, *Fifth Army Corps*, 138; Thompson and Rauch, *History of the "Bucktails,"* 126; Harper, *If Thee Must Fight*, 121; Sypher, *History of the Pennsylvania Reserve*, 265; Longstreet, *From Manassas to Appomattox*, 107; Alexander, *Memoirs*, 153.

CHAPTER 8

95. Although it is unusual to footnote a title, in this case it is necessary. The order of events of Kemper's and Jenkins's attacks is not completely clear. Some authors imply that Jenkins's main effort was first, followed by Kemper's. Most sources point to Kemper attacking first. The author is making his best estimate by relaying the story as follows. The reader is certainly free to draw his or her own conclusions.
96. Alexander, *Memoirs*, 140.
97. *OR*, 763–65, Kemper's report of July 17, 1862; Burton, *Extraordinary Circumstances*, 281; Warfield, *Manassas to Appomattox*, 77.
98. *OR*, 265, Arndt's report of July 7, 1862; 764, Kemper's report of July 17, 1862; Powell, *Fifth Army Corps*, 138; Manarin, *Henrico County Field of Honor*, 238–39; Ent, *Pennsylvania Reserves*, 90.
99. *OR*, 763–64, Kemper's report of July 17, 1862.
100. Johnston, "Charge of Kemper's Brigade," 391–93; Jordan, "My Worst Three Days," 210.
101. Burton, *Extraordinary Circumstances*, 282; *OR*, 407, Childs's report of July 6, 1862; 265, Arndt's report of July 7, 1862; 428, Taggart's report of July 5, 1862. In his report, Union general Truman Seymour was extremely critical of the Federal retreat. He said that the defenders had offered "very weak resistance" and "never should have been driven" from their shelter of rails and logs; *OR*, 403, Seymour's

report of July 15, 1862; Warfield, *Manassas to Appomattox*, 77–78; Sypher, *History of the Pennsylvania Reserve*, 265.

102. *OR*, 123, Grover's report of July 12, 1862.

103. Ibid., 763–65, Kemper's report of July 17, 1862; Ent, *Pennsylvania Reserves*, 91.

104. *OR*, 390, McCall's report of August 12, 1862; Manarin, *Henrico County Field of Honor*, 241.

105. *OR*, 765, Kemper's report of July 17, 1862; 425, Kirk's report of July 6, 1862; Powell, *Fifth Army Corps*, 139; Sypher, *History of the Pennsylvania Reserve*, 296–97; Manarin, *Henrico County Field of Honor*, 242; Burton, *Extraordinary Circumstances*, 283.

106. *OR*, 883, Branch's report (undated); 131–32, Marston's report of July 10, 1862; 133–34, Wells's report of July 4, 1862; Manarin, *Henrico County Field of Honor*, 243.

107. George W. Scheck, *Grand Army Papers*, RNBP, bound volume no. 4; Hill, *Our Boys*, 317; Riggs, *7th Virginia Infantry*, 11; Bell, *11th Virginia Infantry*, 27; *OR*, 765, Kemper's report of July 17, 1862; 390, McCall's report of August 12, 1862; 403, Seymour's report of July 15, 1862; 769, Strange's report of July 15, 1862; 883, Branch's report (undated); Burton, *Extraordinary Circumstances*, 283–85; Sypher, *History of the Pennsylvania Reserve*, 266–67; Ent, *Pennsylvania Reserves*, 91.

108. Burton, *Extraordinary Circumstances*, 284–85; *OR*, 769, Strange's report of July 15, 1862.

109. Burton, *Extraordinary Circumstances*, 285–86; *OR*, 417–18, Stone's report of July 1, 1862.

110. Private Yoder's story is taken from Ent, *Pennsylvania Reserves*, 93–94. Ent cites the *Somerset Herald*, March 31, 1897.

111. Warfield, *Manassas to Appomattox*, 79; Wilson article in the *National Tribune*, April 21, 1887, photocopy at RNBP, bound volume no. 105.

112. *OR*, 86, Edmund Kirby's report (not dated); 92, Burns's report of July 5, 1862; Burton, *Extraordinary Circumstances*, 282–83, 285; Manarin, *Henrico County Field of Honor*, 254.

113. *OR*, 94, Dana's report of July 5, 1862; Miller, *Harvard's Civil War*, 148–49; Burton, *Extraordinary Circumstances*, 285.

114. Miller, *Harvard's Civil War*, 150–51. It is not completely clear whether the Confederates were from Strange's unit or that of Branch. In *Extraordinary Circumstances*, Burton makes the case that they were from Branch, page 287.

115. *OR*, 87, Sully's report of July 6, 1862; letter from Edward Hinks to E.P. Bishop, Colonel Edward W. Hinks Papers, Boston University, photocopy at RNBP, bound volume 180; Captain Rice's report of July 2, 1862, RNBP bound volume 180; letter from George W. Batchelder Papers, photocopy at RNBP, bound volume no. 180; Burton, *Extraordinary Circumstances*, 286–88; Dougherty and Moore, *Peninsula Campaign of 1862*, 51.

116. Letter of George W. Batchelder, George W. Batchelder Papers, photocopy at RNBP, bound volume no. 180; Burton, *Extraordinary Circumstances*, 286. *OR*, 87, Sully's report.

117. *OR*, 111, Hooker's report of July 15, 1862; Gottfried, *Stopping Pickett.* Gottfried quotes Charles H. Banes from the latter's *History of the Philadelphia Brigade* (Butternut Press, 1984); *OR*, 92, Burns's report of July 5, 1862;

unsigned letter to the *Philadelphia Inquirer*, July 10, 1862, photocopy at RNBP, bound volume no. 146.

118. *OR*, 112, Hooker's report of July 15, 1862; Burton, *Extraordinary Circumstances*, 287–88.

CHAPTER 9

119. Lieutenant Frank Amsden was in command of Battery G, as its commander, Captain Mark Kerns, had been wounded at Gaines's Mill, Burton, *Extraordinary Circumstances*, 237.

120. Burton, *Extraordinary Circumstances*, 275–78; *OR*, 410, Cooper's report (undated); 390, McCall's report of August 12, 1862; *OR*, vol. 11, parts 12–13, Jenkins's report (undated), 442; Powell, *Fifth Army Corps*, 138; Longstreet, *From Manassas to Appomattox*, 107; Alexander, *Military Memoirs of a Confederate*, 153. Alexander states that Longstreet ordered Jenkins to charge and does not mention using sharpshooters. This would imply that Jenkins followed orders exactly as he heard them. The truth cannot be known, as it is not certain that Alexander actually heard the orders; description of the terrain from notes by Robert E.L. Krick, historian of the RNBP; Urban, *Battlefield and Prison Pen*, 156–57; Baldwin, *Struck Eagle*, 134.

121. Sypher, *History of the Pennsylvania Reserve*, 268–69; Alexander, *Memoirs*, 153; Manarin, *Henrico County Field of Honor*, 237–38; Robertson, *General A.P. Hill*, 89; Baldwin, *Struck Eagle*, 140. Baldwin cites the *Yorkville Enquirer*, August 7, 1862.

122. *OR*, 410, Cooper's report (undated); 412, Amsden's report of July 3, 1862.

123. Alexander, *Fighting for the Confederacy*, 118.

124. Ibid., 135; *OR*, 396, Cuthbertson's letter to McCall, November 4, 1862; 423, Jackson's report (undated); Manarin, *Henrico County Field of Honor*, 237–38; Sypher, *History of the Pennsylvania Reserve*, 272–73.

125. *OR*, ser. 1, vol. 2, part 3, 442, Jenkins's report (undated); Manarin, *Henrico County Field of Honor*, 237–38; Baldwin, *Struck Eagle*, 134. Baldwin cites the James R. Boulware Diary, June 18, 1862, from the Virginia State Library; Freeman, *R.E. Lee*, 184.

126. Harper, *If Thee Must Fight*, 128.

127. Sypher, *History of the Pennsylvania Reserve*, 268–69.

128. Ervin, *1910 Memoirs of Richard Baxter Ervin*, photocopy at RNBP, bound volume no. 61.

129. Baldwin, *Struck Eagle*, 139–41. Baldwin cites Goree's letter to is mother of July 21, 1862; *Supplement to Official Records*, ser. 1, vol. 2, 443, Jenkins's report (undated).

CHAPTER 10

130. *OR*, 775–76, Wilcox's report of July 21, 1862.

131. Ibid.; 255, Randol's report of July 7, 1862; Hogan, "Battle of Frazier's Farm," 333–34; Burton, *Extraordinary Circumstances*, 288.

132. *OR*, 776–77, Wilcox's report; 421, Magilton's report of July 4, 1862; 255, Randol's report of July 7, 1862; Burton, *Extraordinary Circumstances*, 288; Powell, *Fifth Army Corps*, 142; Manarin, *Henrico County Field of Honor*, 245.
133. *OR*, 776–77, Wilcox's report; Burton, *Extraordinary Circumstances*, 288–89; Griffin, *11th Alabama Volunteer Regiment*, 109; *Chester County Times*, "4th Pennsylvania Reserves," July 19, 1862, photocopy at RNBP, bound volume no. 85; Powell, *Fifth Army Corps*, 142; Ent, *Pennsylvania Reserves*, 94; Manarin, *Henrico County Field of Honor*, 247; Sypher, *History of the Pennsylvania Reserve*, 272.
134. *OR*, 255–56, Randol's report of July 7, 1862; 421, Magilton's report of July 4, 1862; Sypher, *History of the Pennsylvania Reserve*, 272; Powell, *Fifth Army Corps*, 142. There is a lack of clarity about exactly which Federal unit broke directly in front of Randol's guns. In his letter to Porter on July 25, Randol stated that he had thought it was Magilton's 4th Pennsylvania Reserves but was later corrected by Magilton (*OR*, 257). Magilton stated that his men were posted in front of Randol's guns (*OR*, 421) and that they "drove" the Confederates, but later his men "broke and scattered in the woods." It would appear that they were indeed the men who retreated into Randol's guns, but there is a measure of doubt. Such is the stuff of studying history.
135. *Lebanon Courier*, July 17, 1862.
136. *OR*, 776–77, Randol's report; Burton, *Extraordinary Circumstances*, 288–89; Griffin, *11th Alabama Volunteer Regiment*, 109; Hogan, "Battle of Frazier's Farm," 333–34. See the appendices for the story of the flag of the 11th Alabama.
137. Burton, *Extraordinary Circumstances*, 289.
138. *OR*, 777–78, Wilcox's report of July 21, 1862; Barnett, *Yankee Rebel*, 49; unofficial notes in Cadmus Wilcox Papers, from photocopies at the RNBP, bound volume no. 95; Griffin, *11th Alabama Volunteer Regiment*, 110; N.B. Hogan, "Thrilling War Experiences," *Confederate Veteran* 2, 268; Gibbs, *Three Years in the Bloody Eleventh*, 138; Powell, *Fifth Army Corps*, 142; Sypher, *History of the Pennsylvania Reserve*, 273; Burton, *Extraordinary Circumstances*, 289–90.
139. Letter from Meade to Randol, July 12, 1862, National Archives, Military Agency Records, Record Group 153, kk439.
140. Burton, *Extraordinary Circumstances*, 289; Sypher, *History of the Pennsylvania Reserve*, 275.

CHAPTER 11

141. Styple, *Letters from the Peninsula*, 10.
142. *OR*, 162, Kearny's report of July 6, 1862; Burton, *Extraordinary Circumstances*, 291–92.
143. *OR*, 781, Pryor's report of July 29, 1862; Burton, *Extraordinary Circumstances*, 291, 417; Civil War Trust map *The Battle of Glendale, Va.*
144. *OR*, 168, Jastram's report of July 7, 1862; 162, Kearny's report of July 6, 1862; 169–70, Special Order 301, notes on the Court of Inquiry into Jastram's actions, October 27, 1862. Kearny requested this Court of Inquiry (169). The court found Jastram culpable on several counts but took no further action beyond censure.

145. *OR*, 172, Thompson's report of July 7, 1862; 162–64, Kearny's report of July 6, 1862; 781, Pryor's report of July 29, 1862; Jones, *Lee's Tigers*, 106–7; *Lewisburg Chronicle*, December 12, 1896; Burton, *Extraordinary Circumstances*, 291.
146. *OR*, 178, Hays's report of July 4, 1862.
147. *OR*, 177, Colonel William L. Brown's report of June 30, 1862; 163, Kearny's report of July 6, 1862; 171, Thompson's report of July 11, 1862; 172, Thompson's report of July 7, 1862; 177–78, Hays's report of July 4, 1862; Burton, *Extraordinary Circumstances*, 293–94; *Lewisburg Chronicle*, December 12, 1896; Styple, *Letters from the Peninsula*, specifically Letter from A.J. Castater in the *National Tribune*, June 27, 1907. Sponging the guns refers to the practice of dipping the sponge rammer in water and then using the sponge rammer to wipe the inside of the cannon. This helped to eliminate any sparks that might remain. Failure to do this risked a premature firing of the gun and extreme danger to the man loading the cannon.
148. *OR*, 171, Thompson's report; 162–64, Kearny's report of July 6, 1862.
149. *OR*, 785–86, Featherston's report of July 12, 1865; White, "Diary of the War," 123; Manarin, *Henrico County Field of Honor*, 250; Burton, *Extraordinary Circumstances*, 293, 417.
150. *OR*, 870, McGowan's report of July 10, 1862; Burton, *Extraordinary Circumstances*, 293; Sears, *To the Gates of Richmond*, 303.
151. *OR*, 65, Barlow's report of July 3, 1862; 163, Kearny's report of July 6, 1862.
152. *OR*, 163, Kearny's report of July 6, 1862; 61, Caldwell's report of July 6, 1862; 65–66, Barlow's report of July 3, 1862; 67, report of July 5, 1862; 69–70, McKeen's report of July 3, 1862 (major commanding 81st Pennsylvania); Webb, *Peninsula*, 148; Burton, *Extraordinary Circumstances*, 296. In his July 3 report, Barlow stated that the amount of smoke obscured his vision and that he was not certain if the Confederates were in the field or not. He thought they were and that they "fell back hastily at our approach."
153. *OR*, 100, Heintzelman's report of July 21, 1862; 163, Kearny's report of July 6, 1862; Werstein, *Kearny the Magnificent*, 226–27. As for Kearny's legendary meeting with some Confederates, whether true or not, it would eerily be repeated in September at Chantilly, where Kearny would not be so fortunate and would lose his life.

CHAPTER 12

154. James Longstreet, "Seven Days, Including Frayser's Farm," *Battles & Leaders*, vol. 2, 401; Burton, *Extraordinary Circumstances*, 293; Freeman, *R.E. Lee*, 192; Freeman, *Lee's Lieutenants*, 586.
155. *OR*, 842, Field's report of July 20, 1862; Musselman, *47th Virginia Infantry*, 23; Krick, *40th Virginia Infantry*, 14; Ent, *Pennsylvania Reserves*, 95; Burton, *Extraordinary Circumstances*, 294–95.
156. *OR*, 838, Hill's report of February 28, 1863; 842, Field's report of July 20, 1862; 845, Robert M. Mayo's report of July 15, 1862; Ent, *Pennsylvania Reserves*, 96.
157. Krick, *40th Virginia Infantry*, 14.
158. *OR*, 845, Mayo's report; Ent, *Pennsylvania Reserves*, 96–97.

159. *OR*, 850–51, Starke's report of July 19, 1862; 847, report of Francis Mallory, July 12, 1862; Conrad Hansen diary, RNBP, bound volume no. 99; RNBP, map 6b of battle.
160. *OR*, 850–51, Starke's report of July 19, 1862; 842, Field's report of July 20, 1862.
161. *OR*, 901, Pender's report of July 16, 1862; Burton, *Extraordinary Circumstances*, 296–97; Colonel William J. Hoke, *Organization and Movements of the Thirty-eighth North Carolina Troops: January 17, 1862–June 25, 1864*, Major L.D. Andrews's report of July 14, 1862, Southern Historical Collection, University of North Carolina, photocopy at RNBP, bound volume 58.
162. Ent, *Pennsylvania Reserves*, 99.
163. Manarin, *Henrico County Field of Honor*, 262–63.
164. *OR*, 879–80, Anderson's report of July 25, 1862; 838, Hill's report of February 28, 1863.
165. *OR*, 880, Anderson's report of July 25, 1862.
166. Ibid., 391–92, McCall's report of August 12, 1862; 845–46, Mayo's report of July 15, 1862; McCall, letter to wife, July 13, 1862, Historical Society of Pennsylvania, photocopy at RNBP, "Troop Movements" (book subtitle "Penna Reserves"); Longstreet, "Seven Days," *Battles & Leaders*, vol. 2, 401–2.
167. Werstein, *Kearny the Magnificent*, 226; *OR*, vol. 11, 112, Hooker's report of July 15, 1862.

CHAPTER 13

168. Willis Church notes from RNBP file. The church burned on New Year's Eve 1946.
169. Conrad Hansen Diary, photocopy at RNBP, bound volume no. 99.
170. Sneden, *Eye of the Storm*, 88.
171. Marks, *Peninsula Campaign in Virginia*, 331.
172. Black, "After the Battle of Frazier's Farm," 20.
173. Alexander, *Memoirs*, 155; Burton, *Extraordinary Circumstances*, 298; Manarin, *Henrico County Field of Honor*, 266; Tenney, *Numbers and Losses*. In *The Struck Eagle*, James Baldwin estimates the loss to the Palmetto Sharpshooters was 260, page 138.
174. *OR*, 766, Kemper's report of July 17, 1862; 884, Branch's report (not dated); 779, Wilcox's report of July 21, 1862; 770, Strange's report of July 18, 1862.
175. Burton, *Extraordinary Circumstances*, 298; Manarin, *Henrico County Field of Honor*, 265; Tenney, *Numbers and Losses*, 62; Powell, *Fifth Army Corps*, 146–47.
176. *OR*, 111–16, Hooker's reports of July 15, November 8, October 15 and December 7, 1862; 393–94, McCall's report of December 10, 1862. In a November 7, 1862 letter to McCall, Meade stated that he was "greatly surprised at his [Hooker's] account of our doings"; 394–95, Meade went on to say that it was "only the stubborn resistance offered by our division" that checked the advance of the Confederates; 395, Seymour took offense at Hooker's remarks; 395, Porter—in some truth, but also likely to protect his division—said "had not McCall maintained his position on new Market Road, June 30, the enemy would have cut that line of march of the enemy"; 395, James Clark, the assistant adjutant-general, placed the blame on part of the 12th Reserves but said that

other regiments "behaved nobly"; 395–97, further support came from Colonel Roy Stone of the 149th, Captain John Cuthbertson of the 9th, Colonel John Taggart of the 12th and others; Longstreet, *From Manassas to Appomattox*, 111.

177. Sears, *Civil War Papers of George B. McClellan*, letter from McClellan to Stanton, June 30, 1862, 7:00 p.m., 326; Styple, *Letters from the Peninsula*, 115; Baquet, *History of the First Brigade*, 30. Baquet quoted General Michie.

178. Alexander, "The Battle of Gettysburg," E.P. Alexander Papers, University of North Carolina, quoted in Coddington, *Gettysburg Campaign*, 380; McGuire, *Seven Days Fighting About Richmond*, Museum of the Confederacy, photocopy at RNBP, bound volume no. 95.

179. Campbell, "Lost War Maps of the Confederates," photocopy at RNBP, bound volume no. 124.

180. Letter by Cadmus Wilcox, printed in the *Philadelphia Weekly Times*, February 25, 1882, copy at RNBP, bound volume no. 136; Freeman, *R.E. Lee*, 199; J.L. Johnston to Miss M.M. Green, July 20, 1862, Mercer Johnston Papers, LOC, cited in Brown, *Reading the Man*, 323; *OR*, 164, Kearny's report of July 6, 1862.

181. Alexander, *Memoirs*, 155.

Appendix II

182. Bob Zeller, "Glendale Battlefield: A Preservation Success Story," *Hallowed Ground*, Civil War Trust, Winter 2014.

Appendix III

183. Richard J. Sommers, "Joseph Reid Anderson," *Confederate Generals*, vol. 1, 27.
184. Robert K. Krick, "Lawrence O'Bryan Branch," *Confederate Generals*, vol. 1, 119.
185. James I. Robertson Jr., "Ambrose Powell Hill," *Confederate Generals*, vol. 3, 97–98.
186. Anne Bailey, "Theophilus Hunter Holmes," *Confederate Generals*, vol. 3, 117.
187. Ibid., "Benjamin Huger," *Confederate Generals*, vol. 3, 129.
188. James I. Robertson Jr., "Thomas Jonathan Jackson," *Confederate Generals*, vol. 3, 152.
189. Edwin C. Bearss, "Micah Jenkins," *Confederate Generals*, vol. 3, 166–67.
190. Robert K. Krick, "Robert Edward Lee," *Confederate Generals*, vol. 4, 57.
191. William Alan Blair, "James Longstreet," *Confederate Generals*, vol. 4, 94–95.
192. Robert K. Krick, "John Bankhead Magruder," *Confederate Generals*, vol. 4, 140–41.
193. All Union entries are from Warner, *Generals in Blue.*

Order of Battle

194. *OR*, 24–36, Union Order of Battle.

195. Burton, *Extraordinary Circumstances*, 415–19; *OR*, 842, 973–84, Confederate Order of Battle.

Sources

LOC = Library of Congress
RNBP = Richmond National Battlefield Park
USAMHI = Unites States Army Military History Institute
VHS = Virginia Historical Society

Primary Sources

Alexander, Edward Porter. *Fighting for the Confederacy: The Personal Memoirs of General Edward Porter Alexander.* Edited by Gary W. Gallagher. Chapel Hill: University of North Carolina Press, 1989.

———. *Military Memoirs of a Confederate: A Critical Narrative.* Dayton, OH: Morningside Press, 1977. Original printing 1907.

———. "The Seven Days Battles." *Southern Historical Society Papers.* Vol. 1. Millwood, NY: Kraus Reprint Company, 1977. VHS Collection.

Anderson, Joseph R. "Anderson's Brigade in Battles Around Richmond." *Confederate Veteran* 31 (1923).

Baquet, Camille. *History of the First Brigade, New Jersey Volunteers from 1861 to 1865.* Trenton, NJ: MacCrellish & Quigley, 1910.

Barnett, John G. *Yankee Rebel: The Civil War Diary of Edmund DeWitt Patterson.* Chapel Hill: University of North Carolina Press, 1966.

Barnwell, Robert. "General Huger and Malvern Hill." *Confederate Veteran* 37 (1929).

———. "Stonewall Jackson at Richmond." *Confederate Veteran* 39 (1931).

Batchelder, George W. Papers from the Zadock Pratt Papers, Boston University.

Bell, Robert T. *11th Virginia Infantry.* Lynchburg, VA: H.E. Howard, 1985.

Bernard, George S. *Civil War Talks: Further Reminisces of George S. Bernard & His Fellow Veterans.* Edited by Hampton Newsome, John Horn and John G. Selby. Charlottesville: University of Virginia Press, 2012.

Black, A.L. "After the Battle of Frazier's Farm." *Confederate Veteran* 2 (1894).

Cadmus Wilcox Papers. LOC.

Caldwell, J.F.J. *A History of a Brigade of South Carolinians First Known as Gregg's and Subsequently as McGowan's Brigade.* Dayton, OH: Morningside Press, 1984.

Campbell, Albert H. "The Lost War Maps of the Confederates." *The Century* 35, no. 3 (January 1888). Cornell University Library. Photocopy at RNBP, bound volume no. 124.

Clark, Walter, ed. *Histories of the Several Regiments and Battalions from North Carolina in the Great War.* Raleigh, NC: E.M. Uzzell, Printer and Binder, 1901. Reprinted by Broadfoot's Books, Wendell, North Carolina, 1982.

Coco, Gregory A. ed. *From Ball's Bluff to Gettysburg…and Beyond: The Civil War letters of Roland E. Bowen, 15th Massachusetts Infantry, 1861–1864.* Gettysburg, PA: Thomas Publications, 1994.

Coker, James Lide. *History of Company G. Ninth S.C. Regiment, Infantry, S.C. Army and of Company E Sixth S.C. Regiment, Infantry, S.C. Army.* Greenwood, SC: Attic Press Inc., 1979.

Coles, R.T. *From Huntsville to Appomattox: R.T. Cole's History of the 4th Regiment, Alabama Volunteer Infantry, C.S.A., Army of Northern Virginia.* Edited by Jeffrey D. Stocker. Knoxville: University of Tennessee Press, 1996.

Comte de Paris. *History of the Civil War in America.* Philadelphia, PA: Jos. H. Coates & Company, 1876.

Cudworth, Warren H. *History of the First Regiment (Massachusetts Infantry): From the 25th of May 1861, to the 25th of May 1864.* Boston: Walker, Fuller and Company, 1866.

Dabney, R.I. *Life and Campaigns of Lieut.-Gen. Thomas J. Jackson.* New York: Blelock & Company, 1866.

Davenport, Alfred. *Camp and Field Life of the Fifth New York Volunteer Infantry: Duryee Zouaves.* New York: Dick and Fitzgerald, 1879.

Davis, Edward E. Letters, Yale University.

Douglas, Henry Kyd. *I Rode with Stonewall.* Chapel Hill: University of North Carolina Press, 1940.

Dowdey, Clifford, and Louis Manarin, eds. *The Wartime Papers of R.E. Lee.* Boston: Little, Brown and Company, 1961.

Ervin, Richard Baxter. "1910 Memoirs of Richard Baxter Ervin, 6th S.C. Infantry." Photocopy in RNBP, bound volume no. 61.

Franklin, William B. "Rear-Guard Fighting During the Change of Base." *Battles & Leaders of the Civil War: The Struggle Intensifies.* Vol. 2. Secaucus, NJ: Castle, n.d.

Gunn, Ralph White. *24th Virginia Infantry.* Lynchburg, VA: H.E. Howard, 1987.

Hill, Alonzo F. *Our Boys: The Personal Experiences of a Soldier in the Army of the Potomac.* Philadelphia, PA: John E. Potter, 1864.

Hill, Daniel Harvey. "McClellan's Change of Base and Malvern Hill." *Battles & Leaders of the Civil War: The Struggle Intensifies.* Vol. 2. Secaucus, NJ: Castle, n.d.

Hills, Alfred Clark. "Memoirs of Cap't Alfred Clark Hills." Chicago Historical Society. Photocopy at RNBP, bound volume no. 107.

Hogan, H.R. "Battle of Frazier's Farm—A Correction." *Confederate Veteran* 1 (1893).

Johnson, Robert Underwood, and Clarence Clough Buel, eds. "The Peninsular Campaign." *Battles & Leaders of the Civil War: The Struggle Intensifies.* Vol. 2. Secaucus, NJ: Castle, n.d.

Johnston, David E. "Charge of Kemper's Brigade at Frazier's Farm." *Southern Historical Society Papers*. Vol. 18. Millwood, NY: Kraus Reprint Company, 1977. VHS Collection.

Jordan, J.P. "My Worst Three Days." *Confederate Veteran* 26 (1918).

Krick, Robert E.L. *40th Virginia Infantry*. Lynchburg, VA: H.E. Howard. 1985.

Leech, John W.T. "The Battle of Frazier's Farm." *Southern Historical Society Papers.* Vol. 21. Millwood, NY: Kraus Reprint Company, 1977. VHS Collection. From the *New Orleans (LA) Picayune*, February 19, 1893.

Longstreet, James. *From Manassas to Appomattox: Memoirs of the Civil War in America.* New York: Barnes & Noble Inc., 2004 Originally published 1896.

Marks, J.J., Reverend. *The Peninsula Campaign in Virginia, or Incidents and Scenes on the Battle-Fields and in Richmond.* Philadelphia, PA: J.B. Lippincott & Company, 1864.

Marshall, Charles. *Lee's Aide-De-Camp.* Edited by Frederick Maurice. Lincoln: University of Nebraska Press, 2000.

McCall, George A. Letter to wife of July 13, 1862. Photocopy at RNBP in troop movements book of June 30, 1862, Frayser's Farm.

———. Testimony before the Joint Committee on the Conduct of the War. Photocopy at RNBP, troop movements book of June 30, 1862, Frayser's Farm.

McClellan, George B. *McClellan's Own Story.* New York: Charles I. Webster & Company, 1887.

McCrea, Henry Vaughan. *Red Dirt and Isinglass: A Wartime Biography of a Confederate Soldier.* N.p.: self-published, 1992.

McGuire, Hunter. "General Thomas J. Jackson." *Southern Historical Society Papers.* Vol. 19. Millwood, NY: Kraus Reprint Company, 1977. VHS Collection.

——— "General T.J. ('Stonewall') Jackson, His Career and Character." *Southern Historical Society Papers.* Vol. 25. Millwood, NY: Kraus Reprint Company, 1977. VHS Collection.

McGuire, Hunter Holmes. *The Seven Days Fighting About Richmond.* Richmond, VA: Museum of the Confederacy, n.d.

McIlhany, Hugh. Letter to his mother, July 1, 1862. Photocopy at RNBP, bound volume no. 124.

Miller, M.A. Letter to Jed. Hotchkiss, May 26, 1896. Hotchkiss Papers. Photocopy at RNBB, bound volume no. 19.

Moore, J. Staunton. "Malvern Hill: Some Reminisces of One of the Survivors of that Famous Engagement." *Southern Historical Society Papers.* Vol. 35. Millwood, NY: Kraus Reprint Company, 1977. VHS Collection. Originally from the *Richmond Times-Dispatch*, October 13, 1907.

Munford letter of December 7, 1897. RNBP bound volume no. 177.

Newsome, Hampton, John Horn and John B. Selby. *Civil War Talks: Further Reminisces of George S. Bernard & His Fellow Veterans.* Charlottesville: University of Virginia Press, 2012.

Palfrey, Francis W. "The Seven Days' Battles. To Malvern Hill." *Papers of the Military Historical Society of Massachusetts: Volume I, Campaigns in Virginia, 1861–1862.* Wilmington, NC: Broadfoot Publishing Company, 1895.

Philadelphia Inquirer. Unsigned account of 69th Pennsylvania, July 10, 1862. Photocopy RNBP, bound volume no. 146.

(Pittsburgh, PA) Evening Chronicle. "Our Amy Correspondence." July 11, 1862.

Powell, William H. *The Fifth Army Corps: A Record of Operations During the Civil War in the United States of America, 1861–1865.* Dayton, OH: Morningside Bookshop, 1984.

Rhodes, Elisha Hunt. *All for the Union: The Civil War Diary and Letters of Elisha Hunt Rhodes.* Edited by Robert Hunt Rhodes. New York: Random House, 1985.

Richmond Daily Whig. "From the Battlefield." July 5, 1862. Photocopy at RNBP, bound volume no. 55.

Roberts, R. Biddle. "Pennsylvania in the War: The Battle of Charles City Cross Roads." *Philadelphia Weekly Times*, 1886. Photocopy in RNBP troop movements book for June 30, 1862, at Frayser's Farm.

Rowell, Eliphalet. "Six Months in the Military Department of Virginia and North Carolina." *War Papers Read Before the Commandery of the State of Maine, Military Order of the Loyal Legion of the United States.* Portland, ME: Lefavor-Tower Company, 1902.

Sanborn, Lucius. "Savage Station." *National Tribune*, October 12, 1905.

Schiller, Herbert M., ed. *Autobiography of Major General William F. Smith, 1861–1864.* Dayton, OH: Morningside, 1990.

Sears, Stephen W., ed. *The Civil War Papers of George B. McClellan: Selected Correspondence, 1860–1865.* New York: Da Capo Press, 1992. Originally published 1989.

———. *On Campaign with the Army of the Potomac: The Civil War Journal of Theodore Ayrault Dodge.* New York: Cooper Square Press, 2001.

Settles, Thomas M. *John Bankhead Magruder: A Military Reappraisal.* Baton Rouge: Louisiana State University Press, 2009.

Smith, William F. *Autobiography of Major General William F. Smith.* Dayton, OH: Morningside Press, 1990.

Sneden, Robert Knox. *Eye of the Storm: A Civil War Odyssey.* Edited by Charles F. Bryan Jr. and Nelson D. Lankford. New York: Free Press, 2000.

Sorrel, G. Moxley. *Recollections of a Confederate Staff Officer.* Edited by Bell Irvin Wiley. Wilmington, NC: Broadfoot Publishing Company, 1991.

Stevens, C.A. *Berdan's United States Sharpshooters in the Army of the Potomac, 1861–1865.* Dayton, OH: Morningside Press, 1984 (written in 1892).

Stiles, Robert. *Four Years Under Marse Robert.* New York: Neale Publishing Company, 1910.

Styple, William B., ed. *Letters from the Peninsula: The Civil War Letters of General Philip Kearney.* Kearny, NJ: Belle Grove Publishing Company, 1988.

Urban, John W. *Battlefield and Prison Pen: or Through the War, and Thrice a Prisoner in Rebel Dungeons.* Philadelphia, PA: Hubbard Brothers, 1882. Photocopy at RNBP in troop movements book, June 30, 1862, Frayser's Farm.

Vance, S.W. "Heroes of the Eighth Alabama Infantry." *Confederate Veteran* 7 (1899).

Warfield, Edgar. *Manassas to Appomattox: The Civil War Memoirs of Pvt. Edgar Warfield, 17th Virginia Infantry.* McLean, VA: EPM Publications Inc., 1996.

Warner, A.J. Article on 10th Pennsylvania Reserves, USAMHI. Photocopy at RNBP in troop movement book for June 30, 1862, Frayser's Farm.

Webb, Alexander S. *The Peninsula: McClellan's Campaign of 1862.* New York: Charles Scribner's Sons, 1881.

White, William S. "A Diary of the War, or What I Saw of It." *Contributions to a History of the Richmond Howitzer Battalion.* Richmond, VA: Carlton McCarthy & Company, 1883.

Wilson, G.W. Article in the *National Tribune*, April 21, 1887. Photocopy RNBP, bound volume no. 105.

Wood, H.E. "Black Eagle Company: A Typical Command of Confederate Soldiers." *Southern Historical Society Papers.* Vol. 37. Millwood, NY: Kraus Reprint Company, 1977. VHS Collection. From the *New Orleans (LA) Picayune*, February 19, 1893.

Woodward, E.M. *Our Campaigns: The Second Regiment of the Pennsylvania Reserves.* Shippensburg, PA: Burd Street Press, 1995. Originally published by J.E. Porter in 1865.

SECONDARY SOURCES

Baldwin, James J., III. *The Struck Eagle: A Biography of Brigadier General Micah Jenkins, and a History of the Fifth South Carolina Volunteers and the Palmetto Sharpshooters.* Shippensburg, PA: Burd Street Press, 1996.

Barefoot, Daniel W. *General Robert F. Hoke: Lee's Modest Warrior.* Winston-Salem, NC: John F. Blair, Publisher, 1996.

Bates, Samuel P. *History of Pennsylvania Volunteers, 1861–1865.* Harrisburg, PA: B. Singerly, 1869. Reprinted by Broadfoot Publishing Company, 1993.

Brown, Elizabeth Pryor. *Reading the Man: A Portrait of Robert E. Lee through His Private Letters.* New York: Viking Press (Penguin Books), 2007.

Burton, Brian K. *Extraordinary Circumstances: The Seven Days Battles.* Bloomington: Indiana University Press, 2001.

———. *The Peninsula & Seven Days: A Battlefield Guide.* Lincoln: University of Nebraska Press, 2007.

Carmichael, Peter S. "The Great Paragon of Virtue and Sobriety: John Bankhead Magruder and the Seven Days." *The Richmond Campaign of 1862: The Peninsula & the Seven Days.* Edited by Gary W. Gallagher. Chapel Hill: University of North Carolina Press, 2000.

Catton, Bruce. *The Army of the Potomac: Mr. Lincoln's Army.* Garden City, NY: Doubleday & Company, 1951, 1962.

Coddington, Edwin B. *The Gettysburg Campaign: A Study in Command.* Reprint of Morningside Bookshop edition. New York: Touchstone, 1997.

Davis, William C., and Julie Hoffman, eds. *The Confederate Generals.* 4 vols. Harrisburg, PA: National Historical Society, 1991.

De Peyster, John Watts. *Personal and Military History of Philip Kearny, Major-General United States Volunteers.* Elizabeth, NJ: Palmer & Company, 1870.

Dougherty, Kevin, and Michael J. Moore. *The Peninsula Campaign of 1862: A Military Analysis.* Jackson: University Press of Mississippi, 2005.

Dowdey, Clifford. *The Seven Days: The Emergence of Robert E. Lee.* New York: Fairfax Press, 1964.

Eberly, Robert E., Jr. *Bouquets from the Cannon's Mouth: Soldiering with the Eighth Regiment of the Pennsylvania Reserves.* Shippensburg, PA: White Mane Books, 2005.

Ent, Uzal W. *The Pennsylvania Reserves in the Civil War: A Comprehensive History.* Jefferson, NC: McFarland & Company, 2014.

Fox, John J., III. *Red Clay to Richmond: Trail of the 35th Georgia Infantry Regiment, C.S.A.* Winchester, VA: Angle University Press, 2004.

Fox, William F. *Regimental Losses in the American Civil War, 1861–1865.* Albany, NY: Albany Publishing Company, 1889.

Freeman, Douglas Southall. *Lee's Lieutenants: A Study in Command.* New York: Charles Scribner's Sons, 1942.

———. *R.E. Lee: A Biography*. New York: Charles Scribner's Sons, 1934.

Gallagher, Gary W., ed. *Lee the Soldier.* Lincoln: University of Nebraska Press, 1996.

Gibbs, Joseph. *Three Years in the Bloody Eleventh: The Campaigns of a Pennsylvania Reserves Regiment.* University Park: Pennsylvania State University Press, 2002.

Gilbert, Charles E. *A Sketch of the Seven Days' Fight in Front of Richmond.* Gettysburg, PA: J.E. Wimble, 1880. Photocopy RNBP red book 103.

Gottfried, Bradley M. *Stopping Pickett: The History of the Philadelphia Brigade.* Shippensburg, PA: White Mane Books, 1999.

Griffin, Ronald G. *The 11th Alabama Volunteer Regiment in the Civil War.* Jefferson, NC: McFarland & Company, 2008.

Gunn, Ralph White. *24th Virginia Infantry.* Lynchburg, VA: H.E. Howard Press, 1987.

Gwynne, Samuel C. *Rebel Yell: The Violence, Passion and Redemption of Stonewall Jackson.* New York: Scribner, 2014.

Harper, Douglas. *If Thee Must Fight: A Civil War History of Chester County, Pennsylvania.* West Chester, PA: Chester County Historical Society, 1990. Photocopy in RNBP, bound volume no. 41.

Harsh, Joseph L. *Confederate Rising: Robert E. Lee and the Making of Southern Strategy: 1861–1862.* Kent, OH: Kent State University Press, 1998.

Hartwig, D. Scott. *To Antietam Creek: The Maryland Campaign of September 1862.* Baltimore, MD: Johns Hopkins University Press, 2012.

Haskew, Michael E. *Appomattox: The Last Days of Robert E. Lee's Army of Northern Virginia.* Minneapolis, MN: Zenith Press, 2015.

Henderson, George Francis Robert. *Stonewall Jackson and the American Civil War.* London: Longmans, Green & Company, 1898. Reprint, Barnes & Noble, 2006.

Jones, Terry L. *Lee's Tigers: The Louisiana Infantry in the Army of Northern Virginia.* Baton Rouge: Louisiana State University Press, 1987.

Kreiser, Lawrence A., Jr. *Defeating Lee: A History of the Second Corps of the Army of the Potomac.* Bloomington: Indiana University Press, 2011.

Krick, Robert E.L. *40th Virginia Infantry.* Lynchburg, VA: H.E. Howard Inc., 1985.

———. *Staff Officers in Gray: A Biographical Register of the Staff Officers of the Army of Northern Virginia.* Chapel Hill: University of North Carolina Press, 2003.

Krick, Robert K. "Sleepless in the Saddle: Stonewall Jackson in the Seven Days." *The Richmond Campaign of 1862: The Peninsula & the Seven Days.* Edited by Gary W. Gallagher. Chapel Hill: University of North Carolina Press, 2000.

Lash, Gary G. "No Praise Can Be Too Good for the Officers and Men: The 71st Pennsylvania Infantry in the Peninsula Campaign." *The Peninsula Campaign of 1862.* Vol. 3. Edited by William J. Miller. Campbell, CA: Savas Publishing Company, 1997.

Manarin, Louis H. *Henrico County Field of Honor.* Vol. 1. Henrico County, VA, 2004.

Mason, Jack C. *Until Antietam: The Life and Letters of Major General Israel B Richardson, U.S. Army.* Carbondale: Southern Illinois University Press, 2009.

McPherson, James M. *Battle Cry of Freedom: The Civil War Era.* New York: Oxford University Press, 1988.

Miller, Richard F. *Harvard's Civil War: A History of the Twentieth Massachusetts Volunteer Infantry.* Lebanon, NH: University Press of New England, 2005.

Moe, Richard. *The Last Full Measure: The Life and Death of the First Minnesota Volunteers.* New York: Henry Holt and Company, 1993.

Muselman, Homer D. *47th Virginia Infantry.* Lynchburg, VA: H.E. Howard, 1991.

Naisawald, L. VanLoan. *Grape and Canister: The Story of the Field Artillery of the Army of the Potomac, 1861–1865.* Mechanicsburg, PA: Stackpole Books, 1999.

Pfanz, Donald C. *Richard S. Ewell: A Soldier's Life.* Chapel Hill: University of North Carolina Press, 1998.

Rafuse, Ethan S. *McClellan's War: The Failure of Moderation in the Struggle for the Union.* Bloomington: Indiana University Press, 2005.

Riggs, David F. *7th Virginia Infantry*. Lynchburg, VA: H.E. Howard 1982.

Robertson, James I., Jr. *General A.P. Hill: The Story of a Confederate Warrior.* New York: Random House, 1987.

———. *Stonewall Jackson: The Man, the Soldier, the Legend.* New York: Macmillan Publishing, 1997.

Sears, Stephen W. *George B. McClellan: The Young Napoleon.* New York: Ticknor & Fields, 1988.

———. *To the Gates of Richmond: The Peninsula Campaign.* New York: Ticknor & Fields, 1992.

Settles, Thomas M. *John Bankhead Magruder: A Military Reappraisal.* Baton Rouge: Louisiana State University Press, 2009.

Spisak, Ernest D. *Pittsburgh's Forgotten Civil War Regiment.* Tarentum, PA: Word Association Publishers, 2013.

Stempel, Jim. *The Battle of Glendale: The Day the South Nearly Won the Civil War.* Jefferson, NC: McFarland & Company Inc., 2011.

Sypher, J.R. *History of the Pennsylvania Reserve Corps.* Lancaster, PA: Elias Barr & Company, 1865.

Tenney, Leon W. *Numbers and Losses During the Seven Days 1862*. N.p.: self-published, 2014.

Thompson, O.R. Howard, and William H. Rauch. *History of the "Bucktails": Kane Rifle Regiment of the Pennsylvania Reserve Corps.* Dayton, OH: Morningside House Inc., 2001.

Trudeau, Noah Andre. *Robert E. Lee*. New York: Palgrave MacMillan, 2009.

Vandiver, Frank E. *Mighty Stonewall.* New York: McGraw-Hill Book Company, 1957.
Walker, Francis A. *History of the Second Army Corps.* New York: Charles Scribner's Sons, 1887.
Wallace, Lee A. *17th Virginia Infantry.* Lynchburg, VA: H.E. Howard, 1990.
Warner, Ezra J. *Generals in Blue: Lives of the Union Commanders.* Baton Rouge: Louisiana State University Press, 1964.
———. *Generals in Gray: Lives of the Confederate Commanders.* Baton Rouge: Louisiana State University Press, 1959.
Werstein, Irving. *Kearny the Magnificent: The Story of General Philip Kearny, 1815–1862.* New York: John Day Company, 1962.
Wert, Jeffry D. *General James Longstreet: The Confederacy's Most Controversial Soldier.* New York: Simon & Schuster, 1993.
———. *A Glorious Army: Robert E. Lee's Triumph, 1862–1863.* New York: Simon & Schuster, 2011.
Williams, Kenneth P. *Lincoln Finds a General: A Military Study of the Civil War.* Vol. 1. New York: Macmillan Company, 1949.
Wise, Jennings Cropper. *The Long Arm of Lee: The History of the Artillery of the Army of Northern Virginia.* New York: Oxford University Press, 1959.
Wyckoff, Mac. *A History of the 3rd South Carolina Infantry, 1861–65.* Fredericksburg, VA: Sergeant Kirkland's Museum and Historical Society, 1995.

PERIODICALS

Confederate Veteran. Sons of Confederate Veterans.
Hallowed Ground. Civil War Trust.

Index

J

K

L

M

P

R

S

T

W

About the Author

Doug Crenshaw is a strategic IT sourcing manager who has studied history at Randolph-Macon College and the University of Richmond. A volunteer for the Richmond National Battlefield Park, Crenshaw is also an avid history enthusiast. He is a member of the Richmond Civil War Roundtable and is a speaker, presenter and tour leader. His first book, *Fort Harrison and the Battle of Chaffin's Farm*, was nominated in the nonfiction category for a Library of Virginia Literary award.